THE
COOK'S BOOK
OF
INDISPENSABLE IDEAS

What the reviewers said about Barbara Hill's THE COOK'S BOOK OF ESSENTIAL INFORMATION:

ASSOCIATED PRESS (Mary McVean) 'packed with information to chart a course through buying, storing, cooking and eating food ... finally here is what you need to know, in once place ... no need to search through every cookbook you own ... Any one can cook without a recipe using this book ...'

PUBLISHERS WEEKLY 'Among other things, this title addresses the small practical problems that at times plague the home cook ... and--one of the book's most intriguing features--an appendix listing many common food additives ... at this price it's a bargain.'

CHICAGO TRIBUNE (Jean Marie Brownson) 'We liked (it) so much that we immediately stamped it 'property of the test kitchen' so it will not disappear. This kitchen reference book is packed with all kinds of information that has never been compiled in one book before ...'

American Library Association **BOOKLIST** 'A reasonably priced cornucopia of basic information for cooks ... An ideal reference and browsing source...

MILWAUKEE SENTINEL (Lee Aschoff) '...is a lot of book for the money. It offers loads of information, including cooking term definitions, guidelines on cooking tools and their use and ways to cut shopping time and costs ... '

LOS ANGELES MAGAZINE (Laurie Burrows Grad) 'Finally, the answer to your cooking questions ... A cook's dictionary ... substitutions tables ... and ... nutritional information are included in this handy volume.

Other Books by Barbara Hill Available from Sumner House Press

The Cook's Book of Essential Information

The Cook's Book of Uncommon Recipes

THE

COOK'S BOOK

OF

INDISPENSABLE IDEAS

A Kitchen Sourcebook

by

Barbara Hill

Sumner House Press
Kennewick, Washington

First printing 1988

Although the author and publisher have exhaustively researched all sources to ensure the accuracy and completeness of the information contained in this book, we assume no responsibility for errors, inaccuracies, omissions, or any inconsistency herein. Any slights of people or organizations are unintentional. Readers should use their own judgment and/or consult their personal physician or a nutritional counselor for specific application of the nutritional information included.

Since this book was written primarily for readers whose native language is English, and since the diacritical (accent) marks that appear on foreign words do little to assist these readers with pronunciation, the accent marks have been intentionally omitted from the book. Instead, a Pronunciation Guide for most of these and other foreign words and phrases in this book will be found following Chapter 8.

Library of Congress Card Number: 87-060666 CIP participant

ISBN: 0-940367-11-4

Printed in the United States of America

We may live without poetry, music and art;

We may live without conscience and live without heart;

We may live without friends; we may live without books;

But civilized man cannot live without cooks.

Edward Bulwer Lytton
1831-1891

TABLE OF CONTENTS

TABLE OF CONTENTS

LIST OF TABLES

LIST OF TABLES

TABLE OF INDISPENSABLE IDEAS

TABLE OF INDISPENSABLE IDEAS

Chapter 1:

SPICES, HERBS, AND FLAVORINGS IN YOUR KITCHEN

Flavor in food is the cornerstone of cooking. Without distinctive flavor any dish is pallid and, to say the least, uninteresting. Flavor is what makes each ethnic cuisine different from every other. It is what makes the difference among similar foods... won ton, piroshki, and ravioli are all basically filled pastas but totally different in taste because they come from different cuisines each of which approaches food in general and seasoning in particular from its own special background.

Interestingly, flavor is sensed not so much by the taste buds in our mouths but by the nose. There are only a very limited number of taste sensations that can be perceived in the mouth: saltiness, sweetness, sourness, astringency, bitterness, metallic, and the "heat" that substances such as chili peppers produce.

Because most of our sense of flavor comes from the nose, food seems tasteless when the nose is congested with a cold or allergies. Our sense of smell is far more sensitive than most people realize. Very small amounts of substances can produce an aroma that we can recognize if not always identify. The aroma is also more noticeable if it is carried in a moist and warm environment as it is in foods.

Spices, herbs, and flavorings have always had a place in food preparation but their importance has varied over the years, and from culture to culture.

Until the easy availability of refrigerated storage and methods for long term food preservation, seasonings were used both to preserve food and also to disguise the off-taste that inevitably developed as the food spoiled.

Although spices were used for preserving and flavoring by all ancient cultures, it was in the sixteenth and seventeenth centuries that Europeans had the spices of the east and the New World available to use in meats, pickles, desserts, and various other dishes as the world opened up to international trade.

In this century, except for certain ethnic cuisines, most western European and American meals were more bland than the meals served in earlier centuries. The advent of the home refrigerator and reliable home and commercial canning practices made it possible for the cook to shop less often but still serve appetizing food while not relying upon spices to mask the off-taste of deteriorating food.

Blandness went out the window at the end of the Second World War. The roasts and pies of earlier decades moved over to make room for pizzas, curries, enchiladas,and stir-frys... and there has been no looking back. As each new ethnic cuisine moved to the fore, we added more dishes and spices to our everyday cooking.

In the year 1986, for instance, according to the American Spice Trade Association, the United States imported 437,162,000 pounds of spices in addition to the 217,540,000 that are produced in this country. That comes to an incredible 654,702,000 pounds of spices in just one year. And our use of spices continues to increase. In 1985 the total was 640,110,000 pounds... this is more than half a billion pounds of spices!

Americans used 2.0 pounds of spice per person during the year 1972, by 1986 2.75 pounds were used. That additional three-quarters of a pound increase in fourteen years may not sound like a lot, but with normal population increases as well as increased use, the projected growth in spice requirements is significant on a worldwide scale.

INDISPENSABLE IDEA

To make your spices and herbs easier to find when you need them, simply arrange the containers alphabetically. Whether you use a rack, turntable, or shelf to store the containers they will be much easier to use if they are arranged that way.

SEASONING AS YOU COOK

As a cook you should feel free to experiment with spices, herbs, and flavorings and not feel that you must use one certain spice with any certain food just because that is what most people do. As you experiment you certainly will not like some of the results you achieve, but you may also discover a combination that exceeds your highest expectations. You'll never know without trying.

You should also remember that each person has a different perception of what "tastes right" and therefore recipes should not be slavishly followed. Season and taste, and if necessary season again and taste again until you have reached the point that your creation "tastes right" to you.

Start your tasting as the dish nears completion because cooking causes chemical changes in the ingredients, and consequently in the way the flavor of the dish is perceived.

Some seasonings are diminished during cooking while others are intensified. The reason for the seeming paradox is this: when seasonings are cooked in a dish for long periods of time they are broken down and their aromatic substances are allowed to be released. When this has occurred the food has reached an optimally seasoned point. Beyond this point, however, especially if the dish is cooking rapidly and without a cover, the volatile oils which impart the flavor are, in effect, boiled away. When this happens other flavors in the dish are also allowed to concentrate which further diminishes our awareness of the seasonings that were added.

As a general rule then it is better not to add seasonings until the dish is at least partially cooked if it is going to take more than an hour to complete.

Remember too that the amount of seasoning you use also depends on the volume that you are cooking. If you already have added two teaspoons of salt to a large pot of soup, let's say, then adding a quarter teaspoon more is not going to make a noticeable difference in taste. If, on the other hand, you are making a cup of spread for some hors d'oeuvres and have used a quarter teaspoon of salt, adding another quarter teaspoon would double the amount of salt and probably be far too much. This is an over simplification, of course, but the principle is one that you should understand because it is the reason why you have to think as you season food, as well as taste as you go.

Other processing also affects the taste of seasonings. Freezing, for instance, can make a dish taste different than it did before it was frozen. The change is brought about because of the crystalline form that the food takes on during the freezing process. In most cases it is better to season the dish as you are heating it to serve. This phenomenon can make a bit of a problem for cooks who like to prepare double batches of a dish and freeze half for later use. The best advice here is to under season the entire amount and freeze half. Then adjust the seasoning on the portion that you plan to serve immediately.

Seasoning is a tricky business and one that is only learned through experience.

THOSE INDISPENSABLE HERBS

Without question, herbs are best when they are freshly picked and used immediately. A pot herb garden is something that almost any cook can have and in the next chapter we will look at various ways that can be accomplished. Even if you have your own herb garden, however, you certainly will not have all of the herbs you would like to use and you will from time to time use dried herbs from necessity. Or you may buy dried herbs because you are just not interested in the process of growing them yourself, or don't have the facilities to do so.

In general, dried herbs are about twice as potent as fresh but that potency is determined by the way they were originally dried and the way they have been stored.

Dried herbs that you purchase in the supermarket have been commercially dried and have been processed in the most efficient way possible. If these dried herbs are stored in a dry and fairly dark area they will last for about a year. Buy dried herbs in small amounts that you can easily use in that time period. Many supermarkets and health food stores have dried herbs in bulk which allows you to purchase very small amounts at a time.

Herbs that have been home dried are not as consistent in quality, but home-drying is certainly something that you should do if you have extra harvest from your pots or garden. If you have a microwave oven available, that is a splendid way to dry herbs... do just a few at a time sandwiched between two paper towels. The herbs dried this way will retain not only flavor, but also color.

INDISPENSABLE IDEA

Dried herbs take on an almost-fresh flavor when you mix them with an equal amount of fresh chopped parsley and allow the mixture to stand for a few minutes before using. The moisture and fresh taste of the parsley seem to resuscitate the dried, formerly green, herb into something much more palatable.

Some herbs freeze very well: parsley, chives, basil, and oregano for instance. Wash the herbs, divide into small portions and wrap each portion in foil and freeze. Put the foil packets in labelled plastic bags and store in your freezer or freezer compartment of your refrigerator.

Some cooks like to preserve some of their herbs and spices in oil with the idea that not only are the seasonings preserved but the cook also is presented with a variety of flavored oils to use. This is an interesting thing to do but not suitable for storing significant amounts.

THE SEASONINGS WE USE

For a moment, let's look at some working definitions.

Most dictionaries define a spice as an aromatic vegetable component (seeds or bark most commonly) that is used to give a pungent or piquant flavor to food.

Herbs, on the other hand, are products of non-woody, soft-stemmed plants and most commonly the leaves are the portion used.

Flavorings are usually considered to be liquid extracts from various sources and can be protein-based (such as beef extracts) as well as fruit or vegetable-based.

Always remember that there are no rules for using seasonings.

There are suggestions about combinations that have worked and have therefore become conventional wisdom but please don't limit your use of these priceless flavor-producers to the conventional.

Who first tried nutmeg on green beans, or thyme in New England clam chowder, or basil in a mixed fruit salad? Some adventurous cook who just wondered how it would taste. The same cook may have put garlic in custard pudding with less fortunate results but trying is what counts and if you are adventurous you soon will develop some "secret ingredient" specialties of your own.

Having said that, what follows is a table of some ways herbs, spices, and flavorings are used to good effect. Where several are given, as is the case in most items, it does not mean that all of the suggested flavorings should be used in the same dish of course. It means than any one, or perhaps a combination or two or three can be used. It is usually not advisable to use more than three seasonings in a single dish because they tend to lose their identity. Certainly start out with not more than that and then try other additions as you please.

SPICES, HERBS, AND FLAVORINGS IN YOUR KITCHEN

WAYS TO USE SPICES, HERBS, FLAVORS, AND SEASONINGS EVERY DAY

APPETIZERS

For:
Add:

Butter Spreads
Chervil, Garlic, Marjoram, Onion Powder, Parsley, Mustards, Saffron, Sesame Seed

Cheese Dips and Spreads
(Most of these seasonings can be used with dips and spreads spreads based on cream cheese, cheese, or sour cream.)
Basil, Caraway Seed, Chervil, Chives, Cumin (ground), Dill Seed and Green Dill, Garlic, Marjoram, Mustards, Oregano, Parsley, Poppy Seed, Summer Savory, Tarragon, Thyme, Worcestershire Sauce

Corn Chips (bake in)
Caraway Seed, Celery Seed, Sesame Seed

Crackers (bake in)
Anise Seed, Celery Seed, Cumin Seed, Fennel Seed, Poppy Seed, Sesame Seed

Cranberry Juice Cocktail
Allspice, Mint

Devilled Eggs
Cumin, Green Dill, Mustards, Summer Savory

Fruit Cups
Cardamom Seed, Mint, Rosemary,

Garnishes
Paprika, Parsley, Seeds of various kinds

Guacamole
Chervil, Chili Powder, Coriander, Onion Powder, Oregano, Parsley, Tabasco Sauce

Liptauer Spread
Caraway Seed, Mustards

Liver Pates
Celery Seed, Marjoram, Mustards, Onion, Summer Savory, Tabasco Sauce, Tarragon, Thyme

Melon Balls
Mint

Mushrooms (marinated)	Fennel Seed, Marjoram, Oregano, Thyme
Pickle Preparation	Bay Leaves, Dill, Mustard Seed
Pizza Canapes	Oregano
Seafood Cocktails	Basil, Dill Seed and Green Dill, Tarragon, Thyme
Seafood Dips and Spreads	Chili Powder, Dill Seed and Green Dill, Tarragon, Thyme
Tomato or Vegetable Juice	Basil, Oregano, Summer Savory, Tarragon

SOUPS

In:	Use:
Bean	Bay Leaves, Cumin (ground), Dill Seed, Green Dill, Mint, Oregano, Summer Savory, Tarragon
Beef Stock	Bay Leaves, Chervil, Parsley
Borscht	Cumin (ground), Dill Seed, Green Dill, Thyme
Bouillabaisse	Bay Leaves, Saffron
Bouillon	Bay Leaves
Cabbage	Anise Seed, Caraway Seed, Celery Seed
Chicken	Cumin (ground), Green Dill, Ginger, Marjoram, Rosemary, Summer Savory, Tarragon
Chicken Stock	Chervil, Marjoram, Parsley, Saffron, Sage
Clam Chowder, New England Style	Marjoram, Thyme, Caraway Seed
Clam Madrilene	Chervil, Green Dill
Consomme	Thyme
Corn	Bay Leaves
Fish and Seafood Chowders	Green Dill
Fruit Soups	Allspice, Cardamom, Cinnamon, Mace

Gazpacho	Celery Seed, Garlic, Green Dill, Tabasco Sauce
Gumbo	Thyme
Lentil	Summer Savory
Minestrone	Basil, Bay Leaves, Garlic, Marjoram, Oregano, Sage, Thyme
Mushroom	Oregano, Tarragon
Onion, French style	Marjoram, Oregano
Oxtail	Bay Leaves
Oyster Stew	Marjoram
Parsnip	Thyme
Pea	Basil, Cardamom Seed, Coriander Seed, Cumin (ground), Curry Powder, Green Dill, Mint, Rosemary, Sage, Summer Savory, Tarragon, Thyme
Potato	Mustard Seed, Rosemary, Sage
Spinach	Basil, Marjoram, Rosemary
Tomato	Basil, Bay Leaves, Green Dill, Marjoram, Oregano, Sage, Tarragon
Vegetable	Basil, Chervil, Oregano, Sage, Summer Savory, Thyme
Vichyssoise	Chives
Soup Garnishes	Chervil, Chives, Fennel Seed, Paprika, Parsley, Poppy Seed, Sesame Seed, Sour Cream, Unsweetened Whipped Cream

SALADS

For:	Use:
Asparagus	Marjoram
Avocado	Dill Seed, Oregano
Bean	Oregano, Summer Savory

Beet	Caraway Seed, Chervil, Green Dill, Thyme
Carrot	Celery Seed, Ginger (ground)
Celery	Fennel Seed, Mint
Chicken	Basil, Chives, Marjoram, Saffron, Tarragon, Thyme
Cole Slaw	Caraway Seed, Chervil, Chives, Green Dill, Mint, Mustard Seed, Tarragon, Thyme
Cucumber	Basil, Chervil, Chives, Green Dill
Fruit, mixed	Basil, Chervil, Cinnamon (ground), Ginger (ground), Marjoram, Mint, Nutmeg, Parsley, Rosemary, Tarragon
Green, mixed	Chervil, Coriander, Fennel Seed, Marjoram, Oregano, Parsley, Summer Savory, Tarragon
Orange	Cardamom (ground)
Pear	Cardamom (ground), Nutmeg, Poppy Seed
Potato	Celery Seed, Chives, Dill Seed, Green Dill, Mustard (ground), Parsley, Sesame Seed, Summer Savory
Seafood	Basil, Celery Seed, Chives, Fennel Seed, Green Dill, Marjoram, Oregano, Parsley, Saffron, Tarragon
Spinach	Basil, Chives, Marjoram
Tomato	Basil, Chervil, Chives, Parsley, Summer Savory, Thyme
Tuna	Celery Seed, Chives, Marjoram
Vegetable, Chopped mixed	Green Dill, Celery Seed, Chives, Parsley, Summer Savory
Waldorf	Mint

VEGETABLES

For:	Use:
Artichokes	Summer Savory
Asparagus	Summer Savory, Thyme
Beets	Bay Leaves, Chervil, Cloves (ground), Coriander Seed, Dill Seed, Fennel Seed, Thyme
Broccoli	Oregano
Brussels Sprouts	Marjoram
Cabbage	Caraway Seed, Cumin Seed, Dill Seeds Green Dill, Oregano
Carrots	Anise Seed, Bay Leaves, Caraway Seed, Marjoram, Mint, Parsley, Sage
Cauliflower	Dill Seed, Rosemary, Tarragon
Celery	Fennel Seed, Green Dill, Rosemary, Thyme
Celery Root	Tarragon
Cucumber	Green Dill, Garlic, Mint, Parsley, Rosemary
Eggplant	Basil, Chervil, Rosemary, Sage, Thyme
Green Beans	Basil, Dill Seed, Green Dill, Mustard Seed, Rosemary, Summer Savory, Thyme
Lentils	Fennel Seed, Oregano, Summer Savory
Lima Beans	Sage, Summer Savory, Thyme
Mushrooms	Lemon, Oregano, Rosemary, Tarragon
Onions	Basil, Marjoram, Oregano, Sage, Thyme
Parsnips	Green Dill
Peas	Basil, Chervil, Fennel Seed, Marjoram, Mint, Rose

Potatoes	Bay Leaves, Caraway Seed, Chervil, Coriander, Green Dill, Parsley, Poppy Seed, Sesame Seed
Pumpkin	Allspice (ground), Fennel Seed, Nutmeg
Rice	Chives, Coriander, Cumin (ground), Lemon, Parsley, Saffron, Summer Savory, Turmeric
Spinach	Chervil, Lemon, Mace, Marjoram, Mint, Rosemary, Tarragon
Squash	Allspice (ground), Saffron
Sweet Potatoes (Yams)	Allspice (ground), Cinnamon (ground), Cloves (ground)
Tomatoes	Basil, Bay Leaves, Celery Seed, Chervil, Oregano, Parsley, Sage, Tarragon, Thyme
Turnips	Caraway Seed
Zucchini	Basil, Marjoram, Mint, Oregano, Rosemary, Saffron, Thyme
Garnish for vegetables	Paprika, Parsley, Seasoned Buttered Crumbs

EGGS

For:	Use:
Cheese Souffle	Basil, Parsley
Creamed Hard-cooked Eggs	Chives, Cumin (ground), Green Dill
Devilled Eggs	Chervil, Chili Powder, Chives, Cumin (ground), Parsley, Rosemary, Summer Savory, Tabasco Sauce, Tarragon, Thyme, Turmeric
Egg Salad	Chives, Green Dill,

Herb Omelets	Basil, Chervil, Chives, Green Dill, Marjoram, Oregano, Parsley, Summery Savory, Tarragon, Thyme
Scrambled Eggs	Basil, Celery Seed, Chili Powder, Green Dill, Marjoram, Oregano, Paprika, Parsley, Rosemary, Saffron, Summer Savory, Tarragon
Shirred Eggs	Thyme
Souffles	Chervil, Marjoram, Parsley, Rosemary, Thyme

CHEESES

For:	Use:
Bel Paese cubes	Fennel Seed
Cream Cheese	Basil, Chervil, Coriander, Mint, Parsley, Saffron
Cheddar cubes	Caraway Seed, Coriander Seed, Cumin Seed
Cheese Sauce	Caraway Seed, Marjoram, Mustard Seed, Oregano
Cottage Cheese	Chives, Dill Seed, Green Dill, Parsley, Tarragon, Thyme
Edam wedges	Cumin Seed
Rarebit	Basil, Chervil, Marjoram, Oregano
Garnish for cheese dishes	Chives, Paprika, Parsley

FISH AND SEAFOOD

For:	Use:
Cod	Fennel Seed, Lemon, Parsley, Thyme

Court Bouillon (for poaching)	Allspice (whole), Bay Leaves, Chervil, Dill Seed, Parsley, Peppercorns (whole), Rosemary
Clams	Garlic, Marjoram, Thyme
Crab	Basil, Tarragon, Thyme
Fish casseroles (white sauce base)	Celery Seed, Chives, Mustard Seed, Parsley
Fish stews (tomato based stock)	Basil, Celery Seed, Oregano
Halibut	Basil, Dill Seed, Fennel Seed, Green Dill, Lemon, Marjoram, Saffron, Summer Savory, Tarragon, Thyme
Lobster	Basil, Tarragon
Mackerel	Basil
Salmon	Basil, Chives, Dill Seed, Green Dill, Lemon, Marjoram, Summer Savory, Tarragon
Salmon broiled	Rosemary, Summer Savory, Tarragon
Scallops	Garlic, Green Dill, Marjoram, Thyme
Seafood curry	Cumin (ground), Curry Powder, Garlic Powder, Ginger (ground), Tabasco Sauce (or Cayenne Pepper)
Shrimp	Basil, Garlic, Green Dill, Oregano, Summer Savory, Tarragon
Shrimp garnish	Chives, Mint
Sole	Chervil, Green Dill, Saffron, Summer Savory, Tarragon, Thyme
Trout	Garlic, Green Dill, Parsley
Tuna	Basil
Creamed seafood	Marjoram, Oregano
Garnish for any fish or seafood	Chervil, Chives, Parsley

POULTRY

For:	Use:
Capon	Oregano, Rosemary
Chicken	Basil, Bay Leaves, Cumin Seed, Lemon, Marjoram, Oregano, Rosemary, Sage, Summer Savory, Sesame Seed, Tarragon, Thyme
Chicken casseroles and pies	Celery Seed, Green Dill, Parsley, Sesame Seed
Creamed chicken or turkey	Celery Seed, Saffron
Duck	Basil, Marjoram, Rosemary, Sage, Summer Savory, Tarragon, Thyme
Goose	Marjoram, Sage, Tarragon
Guinea hen	Oregano
Pheasant	Oregano, Sage, Thyme
Quail	Rosemary, Thyme
Squab	Marjoram, Summer Savory, Tarragon
Turkey	Basil, Marjoram, Sage, Summer Savory, Tarragon, Thyme
Basting sauce for turkey	Cumin (ground), Ginger (ground), Tarragon, Thyme
Garnish for any poultry	Chervil, Mint, Parsley
Sauces for poultry	Curry Powder, Fennel Seed
Stuffing for poultry	Celery Seed, Parsley, Sage, Summer Savory, Thyme

MEATS

For:	Use:
Beef	Basil, Green Dill, Marjoram, Mustard Seed, Peppercorns (whole), Rosemary, Sage, Thyme

Beef braised	Bay Leaves, Marjoram, Summer Savory, Tarragon
Corned beef	Dill Seed, Green Dill, Peppercorns (whole)
Ground meat	Celery Seed, Chervil, Cumin (ground), Curry Powder, Oregano, Summer Savory
Ham	Mustard (ground), Rosemary
Ham glaze	Allspice, Cinnamon, Cloves, Ginger, Mustard Seed, Nutmeg (all should be ground)
Kidneys	Basil, Caraway Seed, Rosemary, Summer Savory, Thyme
Lamb	Basil, Cumin Seed, Dill Seed, Green Dill, Lemon, Mint, Sage, Summer Savory, Oregano, Rosemary, Tarragon
Liver	Basil, Caraway Seed, Fennel Seed, Marjoram, Nutmeg (ground), Oregano, Thyme
Pork	Anise Seed (crushed), Basil, Caraway Seed, Coriander Seed, Fennel Seed, Green Dill, Marjoram, Rosemary, Sage, Tarragon, Thyme
Sausage	Basil, Coriander Seed, Cumin (ground), Marjoram, Oregano, Sage
Sausage, sweet Italian	Allspice, Bay Leaves, Fennel Seed, Garlic Powder, Nutmeg, Paprika, Peppercorns, Parsley (dried flakes), Thyme (all should be ground)
Shish kebab	Bay Leaves, Marjoram
Spareribs	Celery Seed, Mustard Seed (ground), Oregano, Summer Savory
Stews	Anise Seed, Bay Leaves, Celery Seed, Chervil, Oregano, Rosemary, Sage, Tarragon

Sweetbreads	Green Dill, Tarragon
Tongue	Bay Leaves, Thyme
Tripe	Bay Leaves, Thyme
Veal	Basil, Green Dill, Marjoram, Mint, Oregano, Parsley, Rosemary, Saffron, Summer Savory, Tarragon, Thyme
Garnish for meats	Chervil, Parsley

SAUCES FOR MEATS AND VEGETABLES

In:	Use:
Barbecue	Basil, Bay Leaves, Chervil, Garlic, Onions, Oregano, Parsley, Rosemary
Bearnaise	Chervil, Mustard (ground), Tarragon
Butter	Basil, Chives, Parsley, Rosemary, Sesame Seeds, Summer Savory
Cheese	Caraway Seed, Cumin Seed (ground), Mustard Seed (ground), Sage
Cranberry	Mint
Cream	Chives, Green Dill, Mace (ground),Marjoram, Mustard Seed (ground), Nutmeg (ground), Parsley, Rosemary, Saffron
Creole	Basil, Tabasco sauce, Thyme
Current jelly (thinned)	Mint
Curry	Saffron, Thyme, Turmeric
Gravy	Marjoram, Oregano, Rosemary
Horseradish	Garlic Powder, Onion Powder, Mustard Seed (ground), Summer Savory
Mayonnaise	Mustard (ground), Paprika
Mushroom	Oregano

Mustard	Allspice (ground), Tarragon, Thyme, Turmeric
Orange (for poultry)	Anise Seed, Basil, Coriander Seed, Fennel Seed, Ginger (ground)
Piquant	Chili Powder, Garlic Powder, Onion Powder, Oregano, Tabasco sauce (or Cayenne pepper)
Sour Cream	Bay Leaves, Chervil, Chives, Dill Seed, Green Dill, Parsley
Spaghetti	Basil, Bay Leaves, Chervil, Garlic, Onions, Oregano, Parsley, Thyme
Spanish	Basil, Bay Leaves, Garlic, Onions, Oregano, Rosemary, Thyme
Tartar	Chervil, Dill Seed, Green Dill, Parsley, Tarragon
Tomato	Basil, Bay Leaves, Celery Seed, Cloves (ground), Garlic, Green Dill, Oregano, Rosemary, Thyme
Vinaigrette	Parsley, Tarragon

FRUITS

With:	Use:
Apples	Allspice, Anise, Caraway Seed, Cardamom, Cinnamon, Cloves, Ginger, Nutmeg, Almond Extract, Lemon Extract
Bananas	Allspice, Cinnamon, Ginger, Nutmeg, Rum Flavoring, Vanilla Extract
Cherries	Allspice, Cinnamon, Coves, Mace, Mint, Nutmeg, Almond Extract, Rum or Brandy Flavoring, Vanilla Extract

Cranberries	Allspice, Cinnamon, Cloves, Ginger, Nutmeg, Almond Extract
Grapefruit	Cinnamon, Ginger, Orange Extract, Mint Extract
Grapes	Allspice, Cinnamon, Cloves
Melons	Cardamom, Ginger, Lemon, Mint or Mint Extract, Lime Extract
Oranges	Allspice, Anise, Cinnamon, Cloves, Nutmeg
Peaches	Allspice, Cinnamon, Cloves, Ginger, Nutmeg, Almond Extract, Brandy or Rum Flavoring
Pears	Allspice, Anise, Cinnamon, Mint, Nutmeg, Mint Extract, Maple Flavoring
Pineapple	Cardamom, Cinnamon, Coriander, Nutmeg, Mint Extract, Lemon or Lime Extract, Vanilla Extract
Plums	Allspice, Cinnamon, Cloves, Almond Extract
Prunes	Allspice, Anise, Cinnamon, Cloves, Ginger, Nutmeg, Almond Extract, Lemon Extract
Rhubarb	Cinnamon, Ginger, Nutmeg, Vanilla Extract
Strawberries	Cinnamon, Vanilla Extract

BAKED PASTRY DESSERTS

In:	Use:
Cake, Chocolate	Almond Extract
Cake, Yellow	Coriander Seed (ground), Poppy Seed (whole), Saffron, Vanilla Extract

Coffee cake	Cardamom Seed, Cinnamon, Ginger, Mace or Nutmeg (all ground)
Cookies	Anise Seed, Cinnamon (ground), Coriander Seed (ground), Ginger (ground), Nutmeg (ground), Poppy Seed
Gingerbread	Allspice, Cloves, Ginger, Mace
Fruitcake	Mace
Nut bread	Cardamom Seed (ground), Nutmeg (ground)
Pie, other fruit	Anise Seed, Cardamom Seed (ground), Cumin Seed
Pie, apple	Cardamom Seed (ground), Cinnamon (ground), Coriander Seed (whole), Dill Seed (whole), Fennel Seed (whole), Nutmeg (ground)
Pie, cherry	Almond Extract, Mace
Pie, lemon	Nutmeg (ground)
Pie, pumpkin	Cardamom Seed (ground)
Pound cake	Mace
Sweet rolls	Saffron
Tarts	Poppy Seed

OTHER DESSERTS AND DESSERT SAUCES

In:	Use:
Apples, baked	Allspice (ground), Cardamom Seed (whole), Cinnamon, Coriander Seed, Fennel Seed (whole), Nutmeg (ground)
Fruit compote	Almond Extract, Anise Seed, Basil, Mint, Rosemary, Saffron
Cream sauce	Bay Leaves
Egg custard	Bay Leaves, Nutmeg (ground)

Frosting	Almond Extract, Lemon or Orange Extract, Mint, Vanilla Extract
Gelatin, coffee flavored	Cardamom Seed (whole)
Honeydew melon	Cardamom Seed (ground)
Ice cream	Almond Extract, Chocolate Extract, Lemon, Mint
Ice	Mint
Pears, stewed	Coriander Seed, Summer Savory
Rice pudding	Cinnamon (ground), Coriander Seed (ground), Ginger (ground), Nutmeg (ground), Vanilla Extract
Sherbet and sorbet	Lime, Lemon, Mint, Orange
Spice sauce	Allspice, Cinnamon, Nutmeg

BEVERAGES

In:	Use:
Coffee	Cardamom Seed (whole)
Eggnog	Nutmeg (ground)
Fruit punch	Marjoram, Mint, Rosemary, Saffron
Tea	Mint, Anise Seed
Wine coolers	Mint, Rosemary

Approaching the seasoning equation from the other direction, here are some suggestions of ways you can use the spices on your shelves... perhaps try using one in a way you had not used it before...

Allspice	Use in baked goods and desserts, especially good with fruits; use with sweet potatoes, squash and turnips; use the whole spice in pickles, marinades, and spiced cider; use in fruit butters and cranberry sauce.
Anise Seed	Use in baked goods, especially good in apple pie; use in sauces and marinades for poultry.

Basil	Use in any tomato-based dish to soften the tomato taste; use to season seafood, poultry, pork; add to salad dressings.
Bay Leaf	Use to season soups and stews (remove before serving); use in barbecue marinades.
Caraway Seed	Use in any cabbage dish (cole slaw and sauerkraut too); use in dips and spreads, press cubes of soft cheese into the seeds as an hors d'oeuvre; sprinkle on buttered noodles.
Cardamom Seed	Use in baked goods, particularly cookies and fruit pies; sprinkle a dash on cold melon slices; steep a few seeds with the coffee as you make it.
Celery Seed	Use in salads and salad dressings (good in cole slaw); use in meat casseroles, stews, and meat loaves; use in devilled eggs or scrambled eggs.
Chervil	Use in salads and salad dressings; good in cheese dips; sprinkle on green vegetables.
Cinnamon	Use in sweet baked goods of course, but also use with sweet potatoes or squash; good on applesauce and baked apples; stick cinnamon can be used in spiced ciders, mulled wine and other winter drinks.
Cloves	Use in baked desserts; good on sweet potatoes and squash, also good on beets; use in sauce for ham or pork; whole cloves can be used in marinades and of course poked into a ham before baking. You can make a sweet-spicy smelling pomander ball to hang in your closet by covering a thin skinned orange with whole cloves and packing powdered orris root (which you can buy at a pharmacy) around the fruit and spices.
Coriander	Used in baked goods, especially spicy ones like gingerbread; use in stuffing/dressing for poultry; try in a vinaigrette dressing too.

Cumin	Essential in chili, also good in devilled and scrambled eggs, soups and stews (for a Mexican flavor), try in cheese sauce too.
Dill	Green dill can be used with any salad or vegetable; good with fish (particularly salmon); add to egg salad and sprinkle on cottage cheese; good in cream cheese based dips.
Fennel	Use in sauces for poultry and pork; also used in baked goods; use in apple pie or sprinkle on baked apples.
Ginger	Baked goods, especially ginger cookies and gingerbread; try a pinch in a beef stew or barbecue marinade; add to baked beans before baking.
Mace	Use in baked goods, particularly pound cake and fruit cakes; sprinkle on green beans; add to creamed spinach, chicken, or tuna; sprinkle on top of clam chowder.
Marjoram	Use in marinades for meat and meat stews; good in salads and salad dressings; sprinkle on green vegetables.
Mint	Fruit desserts especially pineapple, add to tea and serve hot or iced; good with peas, carrots, and beets; lamb and mint are a natural combination.
Mustard	Ground mustard can be added to any sauce to sharpen the flavor, particularly good in cheese sauces and cream sauces used with vegetables; use sparingly in meat marinades; whole mustard seeds are used in pickles, meat marinades, and salads.
Nutmeg	Baked goods of course, custard puddings, eggnog, lemon-based desserts; also good in creamed dishes (spinach, cauliflower, poultry, fish); sprinkle on green beans.

Oregano   Any tomato-based dish of Italian or Mexican origin; also good sprinkled on tomato slices and in salads; sprinkle on stewed tomatoes, zucchini, green beans or fresh lima beans.

Rosemary   Use with poultry, lamb, and pork when broiling or roasting; add a bit to salads; sprinkle sparingly on zucchini, eggplant, green beans, and peas.

Saffron   Use most commonly in rice-based dishes, also good in fish chowders.

Sage   Used most commonly in dressing/stuffing for poultry, but also used in pork sausage and good with pork in general; try a bit in cheese sauce.

Savory   Use in salads and salad dressings; try in egg dishes and sprinkle on green beans, cauliflower, broccoli, and cabbage.

Sesame Seeds   Used in baked goods both desserts and breads; a nice addition to salads and salad dressings.

Tarragon   Used to flavor vinegar and in salads and salad dressings; also used in marinades and sauces for meat and poultry; add to meat and chicken salads and also in devilled eggs.

Thyme   Used in dressing/stuffing and in other ways with poultry; add to clam chowder and creamed chicken; add to braised pork chops; use in salads and salad dressings.

Turmeric   Used in pickles; can be added while cooking rice (will cause rice to turn light yellow), add to creamed dishes too.

INDISPENSABLE IDEA

To make an almost inexhaustible supply of vanilla extract, put a split vanilla bean in a glass jar (preferably dark glass) and cover with vodka. Store in a dark place for about a month before starting to use. The liquid will be brownish-yellow by that time. As the liquid is used, replace it with more vodka and keep it completely away from light.

SOMETHING ABOUT SPICES

The history and lore of spices is a fascinating subject of its own. Each spice we use has some special story that makes it unique. Without going into a lot of detail, here is a bit of background information on some of our more familiar spices.

Allspice

Allspice is known by this descriptive term only in English. Other European languages use some variation of the word "Pimento" to describe it. The English word, however, describes the flavor of this commonly used spice which seems to be a combination of cinnamon, nutmeg and cloves.

Allspice is available either whole (in round hard seeds) or ground. The whole spice is used as is in mulled drinks and other dishes where it can be steeped and then removed. Allspice is the only major spice grown on a commercial basis exclusively in the Western hemisphere. Allspice comes from a medium-sized evergreen tree that grows to about 30-40 feet tall in Central America.

Before the arrival of Europeans to this continent, the Mayans had used the allspice berries as part of the embalming process used to preserve the bodies of their leaders. During the seventeenth and eighteenth centuries, allspice berries were used to preserve meat carried on long sea voyages and a remnant of that use exists today in the Scandinavian use of allspice in fish preservation.

Anise Seed

Anise has a flavor that is reminiscent of mild licorice. The plant is a member of the parsley family and is one of the oldest of the known flavoring seeds. Anise is indigenous to the Near East and was used in ancient Egypt. In the days of the Roman empire, anise was used as a flavoring for desserts that would help with digestion after those enormous Roman banquets. In medieval England anise is mentioned during the reign of Edward I as one of the commodities taxed to raise money to repair the London Bridge that existed in his day. Today anise is grown in all temperate climates and is available either as whole seeds or ground.

Caraway Seed

Caraway is another member of the prolific parsley family. Much of the caraway seed we use is commercially grown in Holland but the plant is indigenous over a wide area from western Europe through Asia and parts of northern Africa. Like parsley, caraway is a biennial plant and so only produces seeds during its second year. Caraway has a long history of cultivation in Europe... in fact seeds have been found in the lake homes of prehistoric peoples in Switzerland. In Germany caraway has the reputation for aiding digestion of hard to digest foods and is added to cabbage dishes for this reason. Our word, caraway, is derived from the Arabic "karawya", but in many European languages variations on "cumin" are common. Caraway is normally used as whole seeds.

Cardamom

Cardamom is a member of the ginger family and is native to south India and Ceylon where it grows in rain forests at fairly high altitudes. Although it is not a tree, the plant grows to astonishing heights of six to eighteen feet. Cardamom is mentioned as a medicinal as early as the fourth century BC in Indian texts and was an item in Greek trading boats cargo at that time too. The Romans had a lively import of cardamom from India, it was yet another digestion-aid for the eager eaters of ancient Rome. In modern times, India is still our main source for this spice. Cardamom is one of the most expensive of the spices along with saffron and vanilla. Two disparate cultures make use of cardamom on a regular basis: the Arabs enjoy cardamom flavored coffee and the Scandinavians use cardamom as a seasoning in baked goods.

Cinnamon and Cassia

These separate, but in our minds, closely related spices need a bit of explanation. Both spices have records of use in great antiquity... in the Bible both are mentioned by Moses as part of the formula for making holy anointing oil in the book of Exodus. True cinnamon is the dried inner stem bark taken from a bushy evergreen of the laurel family which is grown in southern Indian and Ceylon. What we call "cinnamon", however, is almost without exception cassia. Cassia is also a member of the laurel family but is grown in southeastern Asia. Cassia is taken from both the stem and the branch bark which makes the trees more productive. Cassia may be thought of as a coarser spice than true cinnamon, but it is the one we are all accustomed to using and we would probably find true cinnamon too pallid tasting to seem like our concept of cinnamon. These spices are available in two forms... "quills" or sticks of rolled bark, or ground. The former is used in pickles and spiced drinks while the latter is found in many prepared dishes.

Cloves

Cloves are a member of the myrtle family and are taken from an evergreen tree that grows to about forty feet. The word clove is taken from the French word "clou" which means "nail" and is a good description of the way the individual clove looks. The clove tree is native to Indonesia. Its use is documented in China as far back as the Han dynasty in the third century BC. Cloves were used by the Romans and continued to increase in use and popularity through the medieval period. During the period of Dutch colonial control of what was then called the East Indies, their monopoly of the clove trade was rigidly enforced. The spice we use is the bud of the clove tree which must be picked before it has opened in order to be of commercial value. Cloves are used in three forms: whole clove buds, ground cloves and oil of cloves which is primarily used commercially in such things as tooth pastes and mouth washes.

Cumin

Cumin is yet another member of that multifaceted family, the parsley. It is also another spice that was well known in ancient times. It is mentioned in both the Old and New Testaments of the Bible and popular with both the Greek and Roman civilizations. During medieval times it had many superstitions attached to it... for instance, it was supposed to keep lovers faithful to each other and it was said that if the seed was cursed as it was being planted an excellent crop would result. In modern times it is grown in the Middle East and Turkey. It is a popular spice all over the world, used in India as an important ingredient in many curries, in Scandinavia as a seasoning for cheese, in central Europe as a seasoning in baked goods while in the New World, it is what gives chili its special aroma and flavor. Cumin is used either as whole seeds or powdered.

Ginger

Ginger is native to southern Asia but now is commonly grown in all parts of the tropical world. The spice we use comes from the rhizomes which grow beneath the ground and from which both the roots and stems of the ginger plant grow. The name is taken from the Sanskrit word "zingiber" which means shaped like a horn, because it was felt that these rhizomes resembled the horns or antlers of deer. Ginger was known and used in medieval Europe and taken to the West Indies to be cultivated shortly after the New World was discovered. One of our favorite uses of ginger, in gingerbread, was popular during Tudor times... in fact gingerbread was one of Queen Elizabeth I's favorite sweet dishes and she had an insatiable sweet-tooth. Ginger is used in modern kitchens in three forms: powdered dried ginger, fresh ginger root, and candied ginger which is a preserved form of the rhizome and used in some baked goods and candies.

Mustard

By volume, more mustard seed is imported into the United States than any other spice. We have become prodigious users of this pungent seed. Its name is was given to it by the Romans who used to mix ground mustard seed with the "must" or grape juice extracted from the grapes they grew to make a savory paste that was called "mustum ardens" (hot must). Even before Roman times mustard was used as a condiment and a medicine, (as it still is today in some places). An engaging historical story comes from the confrontation between Alexander the Great and the leader of the opposing Persians, Darius. Darius sent Alexander a bag of sesame seeds with a message that the seeds represented the vast number of men in his army... Alexander responded with a bag of mustard seeds to indicate not only the size of his army but their strength and power compared to the mild sesame seeds. Mustard is used in modern kitchens both as whole seeds (in pickles and such things as corned beef) and of course, powdered.

Mace and Nutmeg

Both of these commonly used spices are products of the same tree. The nutmeg tree is native to Indonesia and along with the clove tree was a monopoly of the Dutch while they held colonial control of that part of the world. Both mace and nutmeg are taken from the seed pods of the tree. At the center of the pod is the round, brown, hard nutmeg. Surrounding the nutmeg is a protecting membrane which is the source of our powdered mace. There is no record of nutmeg being used in Greek or Roman times but by the twelfth century it was appearing throughout Europe and is specifically mentioned by Chaucer in the Canterbury Tales. Currently nutmeg is imported not only from Indonesia but also from Grenada. Because of its fibrous nature, mace is available only in its ground form while nutmeg may be had either ground or whole. To really appreciate nutmeg's full potential for aroma and flavor, you only have to compare the freshly grated with the pre-ground.

Paprika

This colorful spice is manufactured from a member of the capsicum family which also includes chili peppers and the familiar colored bell peppers. The seasoning of choice in Hungarian cuisine, from which we take its name. The peppers that produce paprika are grown both in Europe and the Americas and are processed by first removing the core and all seeds before the peppers are dried and ground.

It is possibly the blandest of spices but certainly should not be tasteless. Paprika should be bright red-orange in color and turns to a grim dirty-brown as it becomes old and stale. The Hungarians have evolved a whole series of ethnic dishes around its use, the famous Paprikashes and it is used in many Spanish dishes, but for other cuisines it remains more of a decoration than a seasoning. Only ground paprika is available.

An interesting sidelight on paprika is that it is very high in vitamin C. Dr. Albert Szent-Gyorgyi, a scientist from Hungary, was awarded the Nobel prize for medicine in 1937 for isolating vitamin C. He isolated it using from the paprika plant.

INDISPENSABLE IDEA

Oven-dried onions can add a rich flavor to stews, soups, and to some casseroles. They are simple to make. Just slice onions 1/4 to 1/2 inch thick. Put a piece of foil on a cookie sheet and place the onions on the it. Heat the oven to about 200 to 225 degrees and slowly bake the onions until they are golden brown. (You'll probably want to have a ventilating fan going while this is happening!) When they are completely dry and quite brittle, remove from the oven and place in an air-tight container. Keep them in a cool dark place and use within a month or so.

Pepper

Probably the single most important spice in the world, and in dollar value the paramount spice imported in the United States, is vine pepper in all of its forms.

The pepper berries are a product of a climbing vine which originated in southwest India but is now grown in many parts of the world where ever the climate is suitable. This pepper plant is of the *Piper nigra* family and is not related to the green, red, or yellow peppers, chili peppers, paprika or cayenne peppers of the *capsicum* family.

The word pepper comes to us from the Sanskrit word "pippali" which appears in Sanskrit manuscripts written three thousand years ago.

Pepper was one of the first commodities traded between ancient Asia and ancient Europe. During the medieval period, peppers were used as a means of monetary exchange and were freely accepted in payment of debts, taxes, dowries, rents, and many other fees. In the early days of the United States, cargos of pepper worth many millions of dollars were brought to New England ports by daring Yankee sailing ship captains. Elihu Yale (for whom Yale University is named) owed much of his fortune to this early American trade in pepper.

Two kinds of pepper are taken from the vines: black and white. Black, the most common, is processed by picking the berries while still green and then allowing them to ferment before drying. White pepper is made from ripened berries which are picked and then soaked in water for several days. After soaking their outer hull is rubbed off and they are dried.

Pepper is available either as whole berries or ground to varying degrees of fineness. Freshly ground pepper is infinitely superior to pre-ground and worth the investment in a good pepper grinder. Pepper mixtures incorporating herbs and other flavorings such as lemon are also commercially available.

Saffron

Saffron is the rarest and most expensive spice in general use for cooking. The slender wands are the stigmas of a crocus plant. Our word for the spice is another that we have adopted from Arabic, "za'faran" which means yellow. In addition to being a seasoning, saffron has also been used as a natural dye and for medicinal purposes. It is another spice that is mentioned in the Old Testament of the Bible and the ancient Greek poet Homer described the early morning as being "saffron-robed". Currently most saffron comes either from India, Spain, Portugal or Turkey. Although the saffron plant is long lived and relatively hardy, each blossom supplies only three stigmas. It takes 225,000 stigmas to make one pound. In an acre full of plants a good harvest would be eight to twelve pounds of saffron. Saffron has a spicy somewhat pungent taste and is available whole to be crushed as needed.

Turmeric

Our last spice is one that resembles saffron in many ways... but not in cost. Turmeric is a dark yellow or gold colored spice manufactured from rhizomes of a plant that is a member of the ginger family and is native to southeast Asia. Possibly the most common place that the western cook finds turmeric is as an ingredient in commercial curry powders... the ingredient that gives the powder its yellow color. Turmeric is also used in prepared mustard and in some pickles. In parts of India and other Asiatic countries turmeric is used in makeup. India is the greatest producer of this spice but it also grown in parts of South America. Turmeric is available only as a powder.

SPICE BLENDS

There are a number of special purpose spice blends available commercially but you can make most of them in your own kitchen. There are many advantages in doing it yourself: you can adjust the blend to your own preference, you can prepare the amount that you can use up in a reasonable period of time and you can usually save money by making your own. Here are just a few ideas:

Fines herbes blend:	Parsley, chervil, chives, and sometimes basil and tarragon
Bouquet garni blend:	Parsley, bay leaf, celery tops and thyme (tied together in a cheesecloth bag and removed before serving)
Quatre spices:	Cinnamon, cloves, ginger, and nutmeg
Italian blend:	Basil, oregano, marjoram, rosemary, savory, and thyme
Mexican blend:	Cumin, oregano, and dried red pepper
Curry powder:	"Curry powder" is not used in India. Instead a blend of spices is made up for each particular dish that is being prepared. These blends can contain from three to thirty individual spices including: coriander, cumin, chili peppers, cardamom, cinnamon, cloves, ginger, fennel, celery seed, fenugreek, caraway, nutmeg, mace, mint, mustard, poppy seed, sesame

	seed, saffron, and turmeric. The proportions are varied to suit the dish.
Chili powder:	Like "curry powder" chili powder varies widely but usually contains a blend of cumin, cloves, black pepper, coriander and oregano blended into a base of paprika. Ground hot peppers are added to suit your particular taste.
Chinese five spice:	Fennel seed, peppercorns, star anise, whole cloves and cinnamon stick (all ground together)
Cajun spice blend:	Cayenne, garlic salt, basil, bay leaf, white and black pepper, and ground allspice
Blend for fish:	Basil, bay leaf, tarragon, parsley, and lemon pepper
Blend for eggs:	Basil, green dill, garlic salt, and dried parsley
Blend for poultry:	Marjoram, thyme, sage and rosemary
Blend for tomato sauce:	Basil, bay leaf, oregano, parsley, celery leaves, and cloves
Blend for pickles:	Whole allspice, bay leaf, black peppercorns, whole cardamom, cinnamon sticks, whole cloves, dill seed, and mustard seed (the blend would vary depending on the kind of pickle you are making

---

INDISPENSABLE IDEA

A quick and effective way to make low-calorie croutons is to place very small bread cubes in your microwave on a paper towel. Microwave on high until they are hard (about one minute). The cubes will be dry but not toasted. Rub together some dried parsley, thyme, and basil and mix the herbs with some paprika and sprinkle the mixture over the bread cubes and toss well to scatter the seasonings. The results will be very tasty without the calories of deep-fried croutons.

SPICES, HERBS, AND FLAVORINGS IN YOUR KITCHEN

One more list... this time to give you words to describe spices, herbs, and other flavoring ingredients from some European countries which influence our cooking that you may come across while browsing in stores that feature imported products:

English	French	Italian	Spanish	German
Allspice	Piment jamaique, Toute-epice	Pimento	Pimientode Jamaica	Jamaikapfeffer
Almond	Amande	Mandorla	Almendra	Mandel
Anise	Anis	Anice	Anis Mata-lahuga	Anis
Basil	Basilic commun	Basilico	Alabega	Basilikum
Bay	Laurier	Alloro, Lauro	Laural	Lorbeer
Bergamot	Bergamote	Monarda	Bergamota	Bergamott
Borage	Bourrache	Borragine	Borraja	Boretsch, Gurkenkraut
Caraway	Carvi, Cumin des pres	Carvi, Comino dei prati	Alcaravea, Carvi, Kummel	Kummel, Weisenkummel
Cardamom	Cardamome	Cardamomo	Cardamomo	Kardamome
Chervil	Cerfeuil	Cerfolglio	Perifollo	Kerbel
Chive	Ciboulette	Erba cipollina	Cebolleta	Schnittlauch
Chocolate	Chocolat	Cioccolata	Chocolate	Schokolade
Cinnamon	Cinnamome	Cannella	Canela	Kaneel, Zimt
Clove	Clou de girofle	Chiodo di garafano	Clavo	Gewurznelke
Coconut	Noix de coco	Cocco	Coco fruto	Kokosnutt
Coffee	Cafe	Caffe	Cafe	Kaffee
Coriander	Coriandre	Coriandolo	Cilantro	Koriander, Schwindelkraut
Cumin	Cumin	Cumino	Comino	Kreuzkummel, Stachelkummel
Curry powder	Poudre de cari	Curry	Polvo de curry	Currypulver
Dill	Aneth odorant, Fenouil batard	Aneto	Eneldo	Dill,Tille
Fennel	Fenouil	Finocchio	Hinojo	Fenchel
Fines Herbes	Fines herbes	Verdure Tritate	Hortalizas	Kuchenkrauter
Garlic	Ail	Aglio	Ajo	Knoblauch
Ginger	Gingembre	Zenzero	Jenigbre	Ingwer
Horseradish	Cran, Raifort	Kren, Rafano	Rabano picante	Kren, Meerrettich
Lemon	Citron	Limone	Limon	Zitrone
Lime	Limmette, Limon	Lima, Limetta	Lima	Limette, Limone
Licorice	Reglisse	Liquerizia	Orozuz	Lakritze

SPICES, HERBS, AND FLAVORINGS IN YOUR KITCHEN

English	French	Italian	Spanish	German
Mace	Macis	Macis	Macia	Muskatblute
Marjoram	Marjolaine	Maggiorana	Mejorana	Maigram
Mint	Menthe	Menta	Mentas	Minze
Mustard	Moutarde	Senape	Mostaza	Senf
Nutmeg	Muscade	Noce moscata	Moscada	Muskat
Onion	Oignon	Cipolla	Cebolla	Zweibel
Orange	Orange	Arancio	Naranja	Orange
Oregano	Origan	Origano	Oregano	Oregano
Parsley	Persil	Prezzemolo	Perejil	Peterlein
Pepper	Poivre	Pepe nero	Pimienta negra	Pfeffer
Rosemary	Romarin, Rosmarin encens	Rosmarino	Romero	Rosmarein
Saffron	Safran	Zafferano	Azafran	Safran
Sage	Sauge	Salvia	Salvia	Echter Salbei
Savory	Sariette	Santoreggia	Ajedrea de Jardin	Bohnenkraut, Kolle
Sesame	Sesame	Sesamo	Ajonjoli, Sesamo	Indischer Sesam
Shallot	Echalote	Scalonga	Ascalonia	Schalotte
Sorrel	Oseille	Acetosa	Acedera	Sauerampfer
Tarragon	Estragon	Dragoncello, Estragone	Estragon, Tarragon	Dragon, Estragon
Thyme	Thym	Timo	Tomillo	Romischer Quendel
Tomato	Tomate	Pomodoro	Tomate	Tomate
Turmeric	Curcuma, Safran des Indes	Curcuma	Curcuma	Gelbwurz
Vanilla	Vanille	Vaniglia	Vainilla	Vanille
Walnut	Cerneau, Noix	Noce	Nuez de Nogal	Walnuss

Chapter 2:

KITCHEN CROPS

Tomatoes warmed by the sun cut into mouthwatering slices... corn so sweet and tender that you can spread it with plenty of butter and make a meal... green beans that really taste the way green beans ought to taste... and zucchinis, lots of zucchinis!

Does that sound familiar? If it does, you must be someone who likes to garden and has the time, space and energy to devote to this wonderful adjunct to your kitchen.

If you do have the space, the time and the inclination to develop a kitchen garden in your yard, you can have a bountiful harvest of the freshest and tastiest produce possible. But you don't have to dedicate a lot of time, space, or energy to raise some plants that will add flavor, texture, and freshness to your meals.

A few small pots on a windowsill... or basking in the glow of an under-counter light... a planter or two on your patio or balcony... a small hydroponic garden in the garage. Any or all of these can yield a plentiful supply of good things to eat and cook.

There are many excellent books on gardening and this chapter will not discuss all of the aspects of soil preparation, planting, cultivation, and harvesting that those books cover. What this chapter is concerned with are some "indispensable ideas" about ways you can have a sampling of fresh produce in a small space, using minimal time, and more ingenuity than effort.

SPROUTS... SIMPLE AND SIMPLY WONDERFUL

Probably the easiest things to grow, and certainly among one of the most nutritious, are sprouts. You can purchase special sprout-growing jars and other devices, but you really don't need anything other than some things that you have in your cupboard right now.

You might start with alfalfa sprouts because they are quick and can be used in a variety of ways.

Place a tablespoonful of alfalfa seeds in a sauce dish or other small fairly flat dish and cover them with water. Let the seeds repose in the water overnight and then drain well.

Cover the dish with another sauce dish, saucer or small plate. At least twice a day, once in the morning and once in the evening (oftener if you are at home), fill the original sauce dish with water and drain it off.

In about three days you will have well developed sprouts but the tiny leaves will be pale in color. Take the covering dish off and replace it with plastic wrap and put the dish someplace where the light is good. After a day you will have bright green, delicious sprouts that are loaded with nutrition.

Another easy and popular way to sprout is to use a canning jar. Put the seeds in the jar with water (use a one-to-four ration, one part seeds to four parts water) and soak overnight. To strain the water off, tie a piece of cheesecloth or nylon netting over the mouth of the bottle and drain well. Put the bottle on its side in a dark place and rinse and drain the seeds at least twice a day. When the sprouts are well formed put the jar in bright light to develop the green leaves.

INDISPENSABLE IDEA

Use the water in which you soak the seeds you plan to sprout to water your other house plants. The water is full of nutrients that the house plants can use.

You might be surprised at the variety of seeds that make edible sprouts... radishes, mustard, mung bean, soybeans, wheat, alfalfa. In fact virtually any edible seed that produces a non-poisonous plant. (This means that tomatoes and potatoes sprouts must not be eaten because both are toxic to humans.)

Use cool but not cold water to rinse the sprouts (about 70 degrees or so is a good temperature). The growing sprouts should be kept moist but not wet.

When the sprouts are fully developed, drain them well one final time and then place them in a covered dish or airtight plastic bag in your refrigerator until you can use them.

The sprouts are, of course, most nutritious when eaten raw in salads or on sandwiches but also have many other uses. Add them to a stir fry vegetable mixture or saute them lightly in oil and place a spoonful on top of a bowl of a creamed soup... you'll find a variety of ways to use them.

Some sprouts should be lightly steamed before eating. These include sprouted legumes (beans, lentils, soybeans and peas), millet, and barley. Larger beans should be steamed up to 10 minutes, smaller beans take less time. Sprouts can also be roasted after steaming (300 degree Fahrenheit oven for about 15 minutes). For adding to breads, sprouts should be put through a grinder or blender.

Children will really enjoy growing sprouts because they develop so quickly and so visibly. It is a great way to introduce a youngster to the way plants develop and the pleasure of growing something that can be eaten.

SEEDS TO SPROUT

Seed	Soak Time	Sprouting Time	Length When Ready to Eat	Approx. Yield of Seeds to Sprouts
Adzuki Bean	12-16 hrs.	4-5 days	1/2 to 1 inch	1/4 C to 1 Cup
Alfalfa	5-8 hrs.	2-3 days	1/2 inch	1/4 C to 2 Cups
Amaranth	[3]	2-3 days	1/4 inch	1/4 C to 4 Cups
Barley[1] [2]	6-8 hrs.	4-5 days	1/2 to 1 inch	1/4 C to 2 Cups

Seed	Soak Time	Sprouting Time	Length When Ready to Eat	Approx. Yield of Seeds to Sprouts
Beans[1][2]	12-16 hrs.	5-7 days	1/2 inch	1/4 C to 1 1/2 Cups
Blackeyed Peas[1]	12-16 hrs.	3-5 days	1/2 to 1 inch	1/4 C to 2 Cups
Buckwheat[2]	8-10 hrs.	3-5 days	1/4 inch	1/4 C to 2 Cups
Chickpeas, See Garbanzo				
Fenugreek	8-10 hrs.	3-4 days	1/4 inch	1/4 C to 1 Cup
Garbanzo[1][2]	12-16 hrs.	5-7 days	1 inch	1/4 C to 1 Cup
Kidney Beans, See Beans				
Lentils[1]	8-10 hrs.	3-4 days	1/2 inch	1/4 C to 1/2 Cup
Lima Beans, See Beans				
Millet[1]	8-10 hrs.	3-5 days	1/4 inch	1/4 C to 1/2 Cup
Mung Bean	8-10 hrs.	4-5 days	1/2-2 inches	1/4 C to 1 Cup
Mustard Seeds, See the Indispensable Idea about them				
Pinto Beans, See Beans				
Radish	8-10 hrs.	3-5 days	1/2-1 inch	1/4 C to 1 Cup
Rice[2]	8-10 hrs.	5-7 days	1/4 inch	1/4 C to 1 Cup
Rye	8-10 hrs.	4-6 days	1/2 inch	1/4 C to 2 Cups
Sesame Seeds	4-5 hrs.	2-4 days	1/4-1/2 inch	1/4 C to 3 Cups
Soybeans[1][2][5]	12-16 hrs.	4-6 days	1 inch	1/4 C to 1 Cup
Triticale[4]	6-8 hrs.	2-4 days	1/4-1/2 inch	1/4 C to 1 Cup
Wheat	8-12 hrs.	3-6 days	1/4-1/2 inch	1/4 C to 1 Cup

[1] - Steam before using.

[2] - Difficult to sprout.

[3] - Does not require pre-soaking

[4] - Sprouts mold easily even when refrigerated so they should be used within a day or two after reaching maximum length.

[5] - Sprouts ferment easily during warm weather when temperatures are 80 degrees Fahrenheit or more

INDISPENSABLE IDEA

The best way to grow mustard sprouts is in soil rather than in water. (If you try to sprout them in the way you usually sprout seeds you will discover that they develop a rather unpleasant film that tends to make them look like fish eggs.) For best results, put a shallow layer of damp potting soil in a pie pan or other similar dish. Sprinkle white mustard seeds on the soil and cover them with a layer of dry soil. Place in a bright spot and you should begin to see sprouts in about two days. They are ready to harvest in four days. Cut mustard sprouts can be stored in a plastic bag in the refrigerator for several days.

THE EDIBLE LILIES

Next to sprouts, possibly the easiest and most useful thing to have in a small pot in the kitchen are some edible members of the lily family... that would include garlic, onions, and shallots.

Once you become accustomed to having some green garlic on hand, you will never be without it. In truth, growing garlic is even easier than growing sprouts.

To have a constant supply of mild garlic flavoring at all times, all you have to do is fill a small pot (with a drain hole) with potting soil, divide a head of garlic into its individual cloves, and plant the cloves (point up) in the soil. Press the cloves down until they are well covered with soil but the points still protrude above the soil. Keep the soil moist but not wet and be patient for about a week. The first thing you will see are light green nubs developing at the point. Those nubs stretch out into wands of fragrant green garlic that look like green onion tops but definitely taste like garlic. An unbelievably good addition to a tossed salad, or to chop and scatter over the top of a seafood bisque, or to slice and top a hamburger.

Another lily bulb that is easy to grow is that favorite of the gourmet cook, the shallot.

Shallots too grow indoors, but in general will do better in a larger pot than the one you use for green garlic. They also grow well in combination with other plants in an outdoor planter. Shallot sets are often available at your supermarket in the produce section.

To grow shallots, push each clove down into the soil to just cover the point. Separate each clove by two or three inches because they are more vigorous growers than garlic and will develop more roots. Water well and place in a lighted place. The initial sprouts will appear in a week or two and can be cut and eaten right away. As you cut the shallot sprouts, new ones will develop.

Shallots take very little care and can do well without a lot of water although they should, of course, not be allowed to become bone dry in the pot.

If you want to grow the shallots to produce more bulbs, leave them in place for about five to six months, then pull up the entire plant and cut off the tops. The bulbs may then be dried and stored in a cool place for future use.

Chives are a member of the onion branch of the lily family most commonly associated with herbs.

Chives have been actively used in cooking for centuries, actually millennia because there are records that chives were used in the orient as early as 3000 BC. The Romans were very fond of them and as the Roman empire spread so did the use of chives.

Chives are hard to start from seeds but already sprouted plants are sold in the early spring in garden shops and often in the produce section of supermarkets. When you buy them this way they are usually in blocks about six inches square and jammed with roots. Divide these blocks and spread the roots out a bit before placing them in pots that have good drainage.

Chives are not fussy about light and will do well almost anywhere, indoors or out. Be sure to cut the chives back regularly and use them often because, if flowers are allowed to form, the flavor of the chives changes and becomes a little unpleasant.

Chives can be used many, many ways in the kitchen... mixed with sour cream to top baked potatoes, mixed with cream cheese as a spread or as an addition to scrambled eggs, as a garnish for vegetables, in dips... the list goes on and on.

THE INDOOR FARMER... WHAT IT TAKES

Now that you have tried one or two produce projects, you might be interested in trying something more elaborate. So that you can understand what is involved in growing kitchen produce, let's look at the essentials: light, water, and warmth.

First, Let There Be Light

Plants are truly wondrous. They perform a process we call photosynthesis by which cells containing chlorophyll (the material that makes plants look green) convert light into chemical energy. These miniature chemical factories go on to produce the carbohydrate foods that we require from the inorganic materials available to them... the air, water, and soil. This process continues as long as adequate light is available to the plant.

Light is measured in foot-candles. In order to grow a reasonable variety of plants you need to have at least 2000 foot candles of light available. There are devices available that allow you to measure the amount of light in a certain location at a given time but unless you are getting into this on a very serious basis, you probably can do without them.

Simply find the brightest place possible for your plants. The brightness can be from sunlight alone if you have a well-located, big window that can accommodate a shelf to hold some pots. The brightness can be achieved by supplementing natural sunlight with some artificial light. It can also be achieved by using artificial light only (both fluorescent and incandescent plant lights are available). The bottom line is, however, that it is just about impossible to have too much light if you are going to grow edible plants.

One way you may be able to amplify the light you have is to use mirrors around the plants or wrap pieces of cardboard in aluminum foil and place the pieces among the plants. Foil can also be crumpled and placed on the top of the soil to reflect the light up into the plant.

You might want to consider greenhouse gardening... if not a full greenhouse, then perhaps a window "greenhouse" that you can access from inside your home. In these special environments plants thrive because you can control not only light, but also humidity.

Which brings us to the next essential for healthy, edible plants...

Water... Life's Second Essential

Water is required by all living things. Plants use it as part of the raw material used in the photosynthesis process. It is available to plants in two ways, from the soil into their roots and also through their leaves in the water vapor referred to as humidity.

Probably more plants die from improper watering than from any other single reason. Container plants are especially vulnerable to this danger because they are totally dependent on the gardener's whim. Plants can be killed by both under-watering and over-watering but, without a doubt, over-watering kills the greatest number.

In their natural setting, most plants can survive reasonably well with limited water but weaken quickly when their roots are constantly submerged in water. The same thing happens, only more quickly, in a container. Often the same symptoms (yellowed leaves, for instance, that become limp and fall off) can indicate either over or under watering but unless the soil is dry more than an inch below the surface, the chances are that over-watering is the culprit.

On the other hand, if your container plants are outside and you live in a hot dry area, you'll have to water regularly to make sure they have the moisture they require to survive.

If this sounds ambiguous and you wish there were some hard and fast guidelines, unfortunately no such rules are available. Each species of plant is different... its size, its age, the size of the container and the container's location all affect the amount of water that will be required.

The best thing that the home gardener can do is to learn by experience... touch the soil and see if it "gives" under your fingers. If it does the soil is probably just right. If it feels wet to the touch, you are watering too much, let the soil dry out for several days. If it is hard and resists pressure, it is too dry and should be watered until the water runs freely from the drain hole.

Although many books say that tap water should be allowed to stand overnight before you use it to water, this is not always necessary. As long as the water is acceptable for you to drink, it is usually suitable for using on your plants.

Humidity has a wonderful effect on plants and that is why your kitchen is such a fine place to have a few pots for daily use. In other rooms, try grouping the pots together and placing them on a tray filled with pebbles. The tray will serve to catch water drained from the plants and as it evaporates it will increase the humidity around the plants. If your house is very dry, as most houses are in the winter, spray your plants once or twice a week with a mist of water.

Temperature: The Third Member Of The Essential Trio

Most edible plants are not terribly temperature sensitive and will thrive in about the range we prefer... the high sixties and low seventies during the day and the low sixties to high fifties at night. Be aware though that while your thermostat may be set for these ranges, there can be wide differences in temperatures from room to room, or from spot to spot within a single room.

Particular care should be taken with plants kept near a window because the summer sun can make that area much warmer than the rest of the room, while the winter winds can chill that spot to several degrees lower than other places in the same room. Any reliable thermometer can be used to check these things out.

Remember too that plants don't especially like to be in drafts whether the drafts are warm air from a forced air furnace or cool air from summer air conditioning. They do best in a place where the air moves through normal convection (the warm air rising and the cool air falling) rather that in a place where the air is vigorously propelled by fans.

HERBS: EASY TO GROW AND DELIGHTFUL TO USE

Having looked at the essentials of growing all plants, let's move on to talk about growing herbs.

For the small-time gardener, herbs are probably the most satisfying group of edible plants to grow. They can be grown in a wide variety of places and containers. They are delectable additions to many dishes that you prepare... and so much better when used fresh than purchas- ed dried and who-knows how old. By growing your own, you also can have varieties of fresh herbs that you just cannot buy.

There are only a few things to remember to be a successful herb gardener...

Herbs do well when grouped together either in a large single con- tainer or in several small pots. This is because almost all herbs like a humid atmosphere and by having several plants together they all con- tribute to the overall humidity of their micro-environment. They do well on the pebble-filled tray described above.

Most herbs prefer a slightly alkaline soil so if you purchase potting soil to use, check the label to see if it has a pH of 7 to 7.5 for best results. Don't use soil specially formulated for ferns or African violets because it will be too acid.

Herbs, like most plants, require good drainage through the soil so that their roots do not stand in water. They also thrive if the soil is light and well aerated, so mix commercial potting soil half and half with ver- miculite, or mix two parts soil to one part vermiculite and one part clean sand so that the soil cannot become compacted.

Do not fertilize herbs. They produce the most flavorful leaves when the soil is a little on the "lean" side. Their pungent flavors come from the concentration of oils in the plant leaves. If the plant has excess nutri- tion it will produce an abundance of leaves, and those numerous leaves will not be as flavorful as those from a plant whose leaves are on the sparse side.

Most herbs like a lot of light and will do best if light is available nearly twelve hours a day. This may mean supplementing natural light with artificial light controlled by a timer. When herbs are grown in containers, the containers can be moved from place to place on your porch or patio to take advantage of the best light as the season progresses and the sun's position changes.

Here are descriptions of herbs that do well in containers:

BASIL *(Ocimum basilicum)*. Several varieties of this annual are available. All are easily started from seed. Basil grows from 18 to 24 inches tall. Pinching the top of the stalks back early and continuously will keep the plant from becoming leggy. As a native of the sunny Mediterranean, basil is sensitive to cold temperatures and should not be put outside too early. It grows well indoors but it needs at least 6-8 hours of light daily. Too little light results in spindly growth. Basil takes 5-6 weeks to reach maturity. Keep flower buds picked off or flavor will be affected. Cutting back to base will encourage new growth if there is plenty of light. It can be grown indoors or outside.

BORAGE *(Borago officinalis)*. One of the biggest plants you would want to grow in a container, this vigorous annual grows from 2-3 feet during its growing season. The large seeds should be kept quite moist until they germinate, which they do rather quickly. The plant grows rapidly and has a substantial root system so make sure your container is large enough to handle it. A good size would be 9 inch in diameter and at least that deep. Like all fast growing plants, borage needs a lot of light... at least 12 hours a day. This is one place that some crumpled aluminum foil on top of the soil would be a good idea because the lower leaves sometimes do not get adequate light otherwise. Both the flowers and the leaves are edible but, as with chives and basil, once the flowers have opened, the leaves take on a slightly bitter taste and are not useful. You may want to grow one plant for leaves and another to mature into flowers. Because of its size and light requirements, borage is best grown outdoors.

CATNIP *(Nepeta cataria)*. This is an herb that you may not make much use of yourself (although catnip tea has long been held to be a calmative agent), but your cat will love you for planting it. Catnip is a perennial, something of a messy grower and can shoot up as much as two to three feet (if your cat allows it). You can grow catnip from seeds, from stem cuttings, or root divisions and a small pot of it will keep an indoor cat happy through a long winter. Catnip does best in a light soil with good light and average watering. Catnip can be grown indoors or out.

CHERVIL *(Anthriscus Cerefolium)*. This annual is a member of the carrot family. It is grown from seed and unlike most kitchen herbs likes a richer soil. It also likes a little more moisture than most edible herbs and can tolerate slightly less light. Chervil will grow to as much as two feet but keep the plant cut back regularly until the end of the growing season. In the late summer, if you let the seeds finally develop, the chervil will reseed itself and you will have more the next year. Chervil is happiest when grown outside.

CILANTRO or **CORIANDER** *(Coriandrum Sativum)*. In the spice section of your supermarket you will find the seeds and dried leaves of this plant called coriander, but in the produce section it is frequently called by its Spanish name "cilantro". It is an annual and will grow to about a foot or a little more in height. The fresh leaves are ready to use in about a month and you may either cut the whole plant for use or pick leaves as you need them. If you like the seeds (which are slightly orange-spice flavored and are a frequent component of curry powders), the plant must grow outdoors where the flowers can be pollinated and seeds allowed to develop. Let the seeds dry thoroughly (no less than four months) before you use them. Cilantro likes a light soil, a lot of sun except during the hottest part of the year, and not a great deal of water. Suitable for growing indoors (for leaves only) or outdoors (for leaves and seeds).

DILL *(Anethum graveolens)*. This tall graceful plant is actually another member of the carrot family. It is grown both for its leaves and for its seeds. The plant can grow quite tall, as much as four feet but more typically 2 feet, so is not suitable for indoor cultivation. It mixes well with other herbs though and makes a tall center point for a large container of herb plants. If you are primarily interested in the flavorful leaves, keep them picked back regularly. The seed heads are, of course, a favorite flavoring for pickles. They develop from a flower head that is about six inches in diameter. The flower will appear about eight weeks after the seeds are sown. If you plant in the garden, dill will reseed itself and come up again in the spring from seeds dropped the summer before. Dill likes fairly rich, well drained soil and full sun. Because of its relationship to the rest of the carrot family, you'll find it has quite a long taproot so allow plenty of depth if you grow in a planter. Best grown outdoors.

LEMON BALM *(Melissa Officinalis)*. This wonderfully fragrant herb is not one of the standards for kitchen use, but once you start to grow it you'll always want to have it available. It is an easy plant to grow, almost too easy because it can get out of hand if you don't keep it under some control. Lemon balm likes either sun or partial shade. The seeds are difficult to germinate though and it is probably better to start with a plant already growing. The plants can be grown from stem cuttings or root division. Use the fresh leaves in salads or summer punches and the dried leaves in tea or potpourris. An interesting sidelight on lemon balm is that during medieval times it was used in Europe as a "strewing herb" and scattered over the floor in rooms to act as an air-freshener in rooms that undoubtedly could stand some air-freshening! Lemon balm is best grown outdoors but will grow indoors if plenty of light is available.

MARJORAM *(Origanum Marjorana)*. Marjoram and Oregano are closely related and have similar growing patterns. Both are perennials. Marjoram has a slightly less pungent taste and aroma than oregano. It will grow to about two feet at the most, likes its soil to be quite alkaline like its native soil around the Mediterranean Sea and also, not unexpectedly, likes a lot of sun and not a lot of water. Marjoram cannot withstand a hard frost, especially if it is in a container so if you live where winters temperatures dip below freezing you should bring the container indoors to winter it over. Don't be disappointed if you lose the plant inside over winter though because unless it has plenty of light it just won't do well. Keep the blossoms cut off to maintain flavor of the leaves. Cut the plant back in the fall to keep yearly growth compact.

MINTS *(the Mentha Family)*. Here you have a really prolific grower, in some circles known as a weed... but what a nice weed to have around. This is another herb that is best to start from a root division or stem cutting rather than seed. Mints are available in quite a variety of sub-flavors: spearmint, peppermint, pineapple mint, orange mint (bergamot), and apple mint to name just a few. Most of the plants grow to about a foot or so in height and spread vigorously so unless you have a portion of your garden you would like them to take over, keep them in a container and occasionally lift to cut the roots back. Left on their own roots have been known to grow completely under sidewalks and have plants spring up on the other side in the course of a summer's growth! All mints are most content to be out of direct sunlight, in fact light shade would be their choice. Soil should be quite rich because they are such fast growers, and they like it to be kept moist. In the wild they often grow along the banks of streams. Keep plants from flowering to maintain the true mint taste of the leaves. Leaves dry easily and keep well but fresh mint is undoubtedly the best by far.

NASTURTIUM *(Tropaeolum Minus and Majus)*. Don't be surprised to see that old garden favorite, nasturtium, listed as a kitchen herb. In addition to the visual pleasure it adds to your garden, it also can provide some tasty additions to your table. The nasturtium leaves have a bright peppery taste that liven up a green salad when used in moderation. The undeveloped buds made a quite acceptable substitute for capers when processed like pickles. As anyone knows who has grown nasturtiums, they are easy to grow... almost too easy because the trailing varieties can easily take over if given a chance. They grow in any soil that is well drained but do best in slightly sandy conditions. They are an annual but if planted outside you are bound to have volunteer plants from seeds dropped the previous year. Nasturtiums will do well inside as long as they are given a lot of light. Keep cut back and plant a fresh seed from time to time to keep fresh leaves on hand.

OREGANO *(Origanum vulgare)*. This pungent herb is another native of the Mediterranean coast where it is widely used. Oregano is a perennial that will grow quite tall (as much as two feet or more) if grown outdoors. As a container plant it can be, and should be, kept quite compact. Like many perennials, oregano is a bit hard to start from seed and you would be best advised to start with a growing plant. Plants can be grown by dividing an older plant into several parts. Oregano likes a soil that is kept a little on the moist side but not wet. The more light the plant gets the faster and thicker the growth will be (remember where it comes from!) but it will do reasonably well indoors if it is kept clipped back.

PARSLEY *(Petroselinum crispum)*. This may well be the most popular and commonly used of all the plants we think of as herbs. Although curly parsley is what is most often available, if you are growing your own you can also have some of the flat-leaved Italian parsley which has quite a different flavor. Parsley is actually a biennial which means it flowers in its second year of growth. Because the flowering causes an adverse effect on the flavor and texture of the leaves, however, it is normally thought of as an annual and pulled up at the end of its first growing season. Parsley can be grown from seeds (soak the seeds at least overnight before planting to speed germination), but you might be happier with the results if you purchase plants that have been commercially started because seedlings can be quite spindly. Parsley likes soil that is quite rich, evenly moist, and some sun mixed with shade part of the time. Incidentally, in addition to its flavor and eye-appeal, parsley is quite nutritious, an excellent source for vitamins A and C.

ROSEMARY *(Rosmarainus Officinalis)*. Rosemary is an attractive plant and can grow very tall, as tall as four to five feet over a number of years. If you grow it indoors, however, you can control its growth with frequent cutting. It is a perennial and will withstand subfreezing temperatures for short periods of time but if your climate has extended periods below freezing, it should not be left outside. Rosemary requires a very lean soil, quite alkaline and light. Its native habitat, along the seashore of the Mediterranean, has accustomed it to this sort of soil. Its original home also causes it to require a lot of light every day to thrive so if you grow it indoors, be sure to provide it with a lot of bright light. Rosemary has a lovely clean fragrance and you will find that you use if often, especially when cooking meats and poultry.

SAVORY *(Satureja species)*. There are two varieties of savory that are of particular interest to cooks: summer savory and winter savory. Summer savory *(satureja hortensis)* is an annual that grows to about twelve inches in height very quickly. It is easy to grow from seeds and an excellent plant to grow in an outdoor container on your porch, patio or balcony. During a spring-summer-fall period you can plant, grow, and harvest several cycles of the plant. Summer savory likes a rich soil that is mixed with vermiculite to keep it from packing down, and full sun. Winter savory *(satureja montana)* is perennial and has a lower, more sprawling growth pattern. It prefers a sandy soil that is very well drained. Winter savory is rather difficult to start from seeds and is another perennial that you would probably do best to buy already started. The leaves from both species can be used either fresh or dried. Winter savory has a stronger flavor than summer savory.

TARRAGON *(Artemesia dracunculus)*. Although there are a number of varieties of tarragon, the one used in the kitchen is French tarragon. It is a perennial that will withstand temperatures as low as minus 10 degrees Fahrenheit for short periods. Tarragon is a plant that is virtually never grown from seeds because the seeds it produces are just not viable under normal conditions. Instead it is cloned from root cuttings which can be taken when the plant is two or three years old. Be sure to leave at least two or three shoots attached to each root portion to ensure future growth. Tarragon grows to about a foot or so in height and will do well indoors under adequate artificial light. Tarragon is not fussy about soil but does like plenty of light and does not like to be over watered. This is one herb whose leaves are best preserved by freezing rather than drying.

THYME *(Thymus* species). The name of this herb comes to us via Middle English where it acquired its spelling (thyme) and its pronunciation (time). There are several varieties of thyme that have a place among your culinary herbs each with its own special aroma and flavor. Some you may want to consider include lemon thyme *(T. citriodorus)* which is wonderfully lemon-scented and a pretty leaf with yellow markings, apple thyme *(T. odoratissimus)* with its unmistakable apple fragrance, caraway thyme *(T. herba-barona)*, and others. The most popular thyme, however, is your old favorite common thyme *(T. vulgaris)*. Common thyme is easily grown from seed and is a good container plant. It likes a light soil and likes to be kept fairly dry most of the time. To keep it from spreading too much, cut the tips of the growth back regularly to use in cooking.

Herbs are a intriguing hobby. If you find you enjoy growing them, by all means get some books and learn more about their history and cultivation. There are many excellent books, both new and old, about herbs, some emphasizing the horticultural aspects of herbs and others the cultural, but all equally fascinating.

HERBS--AND BEYOND

Herbs are only a few of the things you can grow in minimum space. When the cold winds howl in January and February, order yourself some seed catalogs and look at all of the miniature varieties that are available and "engineered" specially for container growing. If nothing else, plant a cherry tomato plant just for the fun of picking and eating the tomatoes right off the plant. (Sweet Hundreds is a variety that does particularly well and has a delightful flavor.)

INDISPENSABLE IDEA

Consider growing lettuce indoors in the winter. There are a number of miniature varieties that are suitable. Plant the seed in two parts potting soil mixed with one part vermiculite. Seeds should be planted according to package directions and kept cool and moist until they sprout. Plant dwarf varieties about 4-5 inches apart. If you leave the root in the soil and undamaged the plants will continue to send up fresh leaves after each picking.

Gardening can be a hobby that the whole family can enjoy. Children are captivated by the idea that a tiny seed they can hardly see can develop into a plant as big as they are and furthermore produce something that they can enjoy eating too. Even if you don't have the space to have an large outside garden, encourage the children to participate in small scale edible plant raising plans and perhaps have a container or two of their own. The fast germinating plants such as radishes and lettuce make a good starting point for young gardeners.

Another plant project for young gardeners is the tried and true sweet potato (or yam) vine. Simply get the child together with a sweet potato or yam, a quart jar with a wide mouth and about four or five toothpicks.

You remember how it works... place the toothpicks around the center of the potato at regular intervals and then submerge about half of the potato in the water and put it in a spot away from direct light. Shortly your potato will sprout both roots and leaves in a very satisfying way.

When the leaf shoots are about six inches long, the tuber can be transplanted to soil to continue its growth. When they are grown commercially for food, the soil is kept light so that the tubers can easily attain full growth without fighting their way through the soil. For a decorative vine with maximum leaf growth use a good rich commercial potting soil.

Incidentally, use a larger container than you might originally think because these plants really put out the roots. Like most quick growing plants they like to have plenty of water so keep the soil evenly moist all the time. Keep them in a sunny spot and in no time you will have a window full of vines... and maybe even some flowers.

You should be aware that some sweet potatoes and yams you purchase at your supermarket have been treated to retard sprouting so if the first one you try doesn't respond with sprouts within about two weeks, try another one.

INDISPENSABLE IDEA

If you can't stand throwing out that beautiful avocado seed, here are some suggestions to insure a healthy plant. Cut a very thin sliver from the top and bottom of the seed (not more than an eighth of an inch and use a sharp knife). Plant it with the large end down and about two-thirds covered with planting soil. Water well and cover the top of the seed with a glass to keep the humidity around it high. Be patient and wait for the seed to split. When it does cover it with soil and let the plant grow. When it reaches six inches in height cut off the top two inches and you will keep it from growing too tall and spindly and instead force it to push out several branches. When you first trim it back it will look forlorn but soon new branches will develop and you will have the beginning of a lovely plant.

Here are some final "indispensable ideas" for successful container gardening, especially indoor container gardening...

Light...

Plants like light. Indoors it is almost impossible to give a plant too much light. You'll find that plants "reach" for the light which results in long stems and sparse leaves. On the other hand, if your containers are outdoors, be guided by the plant's preference for light or semi-shade.

Try to duplicate the plant's natural growing conditions as closely as you can... forest floor herbs feel most at home in a shady environment while herbs from the dry and sunny Mediterranean coast like to bask in the sun all day.

When you bring your containers indoors at the end of the summer or take them out in the spring, remember that this is a major change for the plant and allow it a little time to adjust... it may drop a few leaves when you bring it in for instance (a plant's way of registering surprise at a change in its life... remember plants are not the mobile creatures that animals are and any change is a major one for a plant!).

Watering...

Use water that is at room temperature, or even a little warmer. Most plants, like most people, are not fond of cold baths and there is some research to indicate that plants grow faster and more productively when warm water is used for irrigation (that is to say, watering!).

If you have a choice, watering in the evening is probably preferable because it duplicates the pattern of dew accumulation at night. If your plants are in the direct sun, drops of water on the leaves can act as tiny lenses and actually cause burning by focusing light beams on tender leaf tissue.

Water less often rather than more often. This is a little tricky because each plant's requirement is different. But unless it is very hot and dry and plants are transpiring heavily (and this would be plants in containers outdoors), watering every day is usually not a good idea for several reasons. The plant roots stay too wet, and oxygen which roots need is forced out of the soil. Furthermore, because the water is always near the surface, the roots do not push down into the container so the plant is not as strong and more subject to root rot than a plant whose roots are strong and healthy.

If your water is heavily chlorinated, you may want to fill a container and let it stand for 24 hours to let the chlorine evaporate before using to water the plants, but in most cases tap water is acceptable.

Don't use artificially softened water on your plants. The salts used to soften the water accumulate in the soil and are not good for the plant at all. Water softeners are usually attached to the hot water line in your home.

When you are going to be away on a trip, you need to make some plans for your plants as well as yourself. If you have a neighbor or friend who can come in and water them that is ideal but if that can't be worked out, you will need to make some other arrangements.

Most plants, except the very tender, can easily go for a week without water.

If you will be away longer than that, there are a variety of things you can do depending on the plant, where you have it growing, and how long you will be gone.

Indoor plants can be watered well then covered with a large plastic bag which is tied around the pot and will hold in the humidity (don't put plastic bagged plants in direct sunlight though or they may have leaf burn when you return). You can also put a layer of wet newspapers in your bathtub and arrange containers on it (this works particularly well if you can leave your bathroom light on or have it on a timer).

Outdoor container plants are more of a problem because they usually require more water. One thing that works very well is a drip watering arrangement that you can purchase at most hardware or garden stores. These systems, while not expensive, take a bit of effort and planning to install, but once in you can use them as an automatic watering system all the time and save yourself a lot of effort.

Soil...

In general you will have much better results if you use a commercial potting soil for your containers rather than garden soil. Commercial soil is a balanced mixture and is free from bugs and bacteria... something that you cannot say about soil from your yard. Mixing the bagged potting soil with vermiculite (2 parts soil to one part vermiculite) will lighten the soil and give it better drainage. It will also help keep the weight of the containers down.

Just as a farmer cultivates his crops, you will have healthier plants if you "cultivate" the soil in your containers by stirring it up gently with a gardening fork (or an old carving fork). Go gently so you don't damage the tender roots but by turning the soil occasionally you will bring in oxygen that the roots need to grow.

When a perennial herb has remained in the same pot for two or three years, it is time for fresh soil. Tip it out gently and tap the old soil out of the pot. This is a good time to prune the roots if they are becoming root-bound in the pot. Gently pry the root ball apart and spread the roots out a bit. Put a layer of fresh soil in the bottom of the pot and then replace the plant and gently press fresh soil around the roots. Make sure that the roots are all in contact with the soil. Fill the container and give the plant a good watering to settle the new soil.

Fertilizers...

This is another area of individual plant preference. Herbs in general are most flavorful when they are not over-fertilized and for most of them that means no fertilizer at all. Check information on the individual herbs to see what each one specifically needs.

For plants that do take fertilizer, two suggestions... vary the fertilizer you use (variety is good for everything, including your plants), and keep the fertilizer diluted. There is a great temptation to "be nice" to our plants and give them "a lot to eat"... unfortunately this "tender loving care" is a little misplaced in this particular instance and the plants will be happier and healthier if they are fed moderately on a regular schedule.

"Natural" fertilizers are good to use because they break down slowly in the soil. Fish fertilizer doesn't have the greatest aroma in the world but it is a fine source of nitrogen in a slow release form. Occasionally soak egg shells in water and use the water on your plants to add valuable nutrients to the soil.

For those of you who are able to have an outdoor yard garden full of the tomatoes, green beans, and zucchini mentioned at the beginning of this chapter, here is a list of what you can expect in terms of maturing time for some of the most popular home garden crops. Remember that the fast growing plants will allow you to have more than one planting during most growing seasons in most of the moderate climate areas.

KITCHEN CROPS

VEGETABLE PLANTING AND HARVEST SCHEDULE

(These are only estimates to help you plan, the dates are based on a last frost in mid-March and a first frost in mid-October. Adjust the dates to fit your particular climate and location.)

Vegetable	Plant in	To Harvest in
Beans, fresh	May	July
	July	September
Beets	April	July
	August	October
Broccoli	March	June
	July	October
Brussels Sprouts	July	October
Cabbage	March	July
Carrots	April	June
	July	October
Corn	May	August
Cucumber	May	July
	June	August
	August	September
Endive	March	June
	July	October
Lettuce	March	April
	April	May
	May	June
	August	September
	September	October
Onions, green	April	May
Onions	April	August
Peas	March	May
	April	June
Peas, snow (pods)	April	June
	June	August
Peppers	April	July
Radishes	April	May
	May	June
Swiss chard	April	July
Tomatoes	May	September
Turnips	March	May
	August	October

INDISPENSABLE IDEA

To remove the skin from a lot of tomatoes at one time, bring a large kettle of water to a slow boil, place the tomatoes in the basket you use in your French frier and lower the basket into the boiling water for a couple of minutes. Don't overload the basket because the water has to reach all parts of each tomato.

Chapter 3:

TAKE AWAY MEALS... PICNICS PLUS

Let's go camping... let's take the boat out... let's go to the park or the beach for a picnic... let's go biking... let's go to the game (and take something to eat!)... let's go cross-country skiing... let's rent a vacation condo...

Or on a more Monday-to-Friday basis... let's take a "brown bag" to work or school.

We eat a lot of meals away from home that are prepared in our own kitchens and not in a restaurant. Lunches taken to work or to school can, thanks to thermos containers and insulated bags, include as much variety as the person eating the lunch would like to have. Let's not forget, in our effort to bring variety to carry-out lunches, however, that lots of people, especially kids, really like peanut butter-and-jelly and really like to have it almost every day.

Since what we prepare depends largely on when and where we are going to be eating it, let's look at some of the categories separately. And let's keep in mind that, except for school and work, these excursions are for fun, relaxation and recreation... so allow yourself to have fun, relax, and "recreate".

CAMPING AND "MOBILING"

The most elaborate plans have to be made when you will be gone for more than a day on a camping trip or in the mobile "camp" of your camper, trailer or motor home.

Plans like these imply that you will have a certain place where food will be prepared for the length of time you are away from home. This place can center around an open fire, although with fire restrictions this is less common now than it once was, or center around a camp stove or the stove in your mobile environment.

There are some overall principles to keep in mind in planning this sort of trip from a food preparation standpoint:

1. Take along kitchen equipment that can be used for more than one job.

This is not the place for the special nutmeg grater or four-piece mixing bowl set no matter how indispensable they are at home. Instead take small multipurpose pieces: a knife with a blade long enough to cut bread and slice meat, but short enough to use as a paring knife, a flat grater that can be used to coarse grate cheese, fine grate boiled eggs, and slice cheese (maybe even grate whole nutmegs if you find the right grater!), a wine bottle empty or full makes a fine rolling pin too.

Don't forget that table service silver can also do double duty in food preparation (forks can whip scrambled eggs, spoons can double as measuring spoons if you try them out at home first to see what equals what).

2. Take as little as possible. If there ever is a place where "simplest is best" an away-from-home trip is that place. Ask the question, can we possibly get along without it? If the answer is "yes" or even "maybe", leave it home. There is a school of thought that says it is better to have it and not need it than to need it and not have it... people who belong to that school of thought should be the ones responsible for packing, carrying, and unpacking during the entire trip... their philosophy will very likely change.

Here is a suggested list of things you probably will want to take however:

Cooking utensils:

Large, flat-bottomed kettle (8 quart capacity) with lid. (Use the kettle to carry other kitchen equipment)

Medium-sized saucepan (about 2 quart capacity) with lid

Skillet of a size appropriate to the number in your group

Stove-top toaster

Collapsible steamer (small enough to be used in saucepan)

Serving dishes and silver:

China, glass or plastic is up to you and to the style you like. Plastic meets the requirements of being light, durable, and versatile. The "luxury" of china adds a special style to a camp setting... drinking wine from a stemmed, real glass wine glass adds a note of elegance to the simplest meal. (Of course, glass is still fragile, especially in this setting, so don't take anything you wouldn't want to lose by having it accidentally broken.)

Although sturdy plastic tableware is available, stainless steel tableware is probably the best under these circumstances. A knife, fork, teaspoon, and soup spoon for each person in your group plus a couple of serving spoons should be adequate.

Food preparation and cleanup:

Knife with about a six inch blade

Manual can opener (take a good one, you don't want to be fifty miles away from the nearest store and have your only can opener refuse to do its job).

Spatula of your favorite style

Tongs, a small pair that you can fasten together with a rubber band.

Chopping board, a small, non-wooden board because keeping a wooden board clean will be a problem.

Mixing bowl big enough for salad, small enough for scrambled eggs

Measuring cup that you can also be use as a small mixing bowl.

Corkscrew

Ice pick

Waterproof matches

Assortment of self-sealing plastic bags, plastic and foil wrap

Paper towels that can double as paper napkins and place mats

Scouring pad, dish detergent, and a small basin for the inevitable dish washing

INDISPENSABLE IDEAS

For a multipurpose measuring cup, take a drinking glass and mark on it 1/4, 1/2, 3/4, and 1 cup measures. Find the measurement marks by using a standard measuring cup before you leave home and mark the lines with an indelible marker.

If you have a boat, trailer, or RV, you may want to keep the galley permanently equipped. Your storage space will largely dictate what you are able to have with you, but it will certainly be more than you would take on an outdoor camping trip. These in-motion-homes have their own set of problems though... motion being the source of most of the problems. Make sure that shelves have rails, cupboard doors are kept closed. If you hang cups from hooks, bend the hook so that the cup will not come off easily. You may be able to use small hammocks in some locations to store odd-shaped items or things that might roll around if left on their own.

One item that can be especially useful is a small hibachi and a similarly small but adequate supply of charcoal. There are those times when the stove fuel supply has not been replenished and you know you are running low, or when a barbecued meal is just what you want, or when some hot hors d'oeuvres would turn a get-together of drop in visitors into something very like a party.

But you need to take more than equipment on a camping trip... the other half of the equation is the food you are going to fix. What you take specifically, of course, depends on the number of people in the group and their preferences, but some general guidelines apply.

Here's where some pre-planning and a list or two will be a big help.

First determine how many days you will be gone and multiply that by three (for three meals a day) then multiply that result by the number of people in the group. That final figure will be the maximum number of meals you will have to plan for.

Next turn a large sheet of paper horizontally and divide it into four sections across the short side and as many sections across the long side as days you will be gone. Mark one row "Breakfast", the second "Lunch", the third "Dinner" and the fourth "Snacks etc.".

Days	1	2	3	4
B'fast				
Lunch				
Dinner				
Snacks				

Start with the first meal you will be cooking and plan a menu for each meal from then on. This may sound like a nuisance and as though all the spontaneity of the trip's meals will be spoiled but no one says you have to stick to your plan slavishly... if something happens to change a meal, just change it. Having an overall plan will make sure that if you do in fact eat every meal, everything you need to feed everyone will be available.

This sort of planning becomes less important if you travel away a lot because what to take becomes almost second nature, but until you have a real feel for what you use and what the people you cook for like, a plan just can't be beat. (For you experienced campers an occasional plan might bring some welcome variety into what has become "standard camp food" for your group!)

POCKET AND PACK MEALS

Another kind of getaway lasts for only a day and usually for only a meal or two. The key here is that the food must be completely portable and the lighter the better because it has to be carried "on your person". These trips can be hikes, bike trips, or cross-country ski trips depending on the season.

Pocket foods are the easiest to describe because they are somewhat limited due to the space available to carry them. Here are some possibilities:

> Cheese (you can purchase individually wrapped packets, some are even packed with crackers)
>
> Dry meats (jerky, dry salami, dry smoked fish, commercially available meat sticks... be sure not to take meats that require refrigeration such as regular cold cuts)
>
> Crackers (hard tack is a good choice, avoid crackers that will disintegrate into crumbs during the first hour)
>
> Dried fruit and/or nuts
>
> "Gorp" this do-it-as-you-like-it combination of nuts, dried fruit, chocolate and/or butterscotch chips, coconut, seeds and whatever else strikes your fancy has become a staple for backpackers... "high energy" (read that high in calories), easy to make, easy to pack, and easy to eat.
>
> Candy, wrapped pieces or bars

On a day trip you will not need all of these, but one thing that you will need is water. While water containers are bulky and comparatively heavy, always take your water with you and don't depend on being able to find, or drink, stream or lake water along the way. If you fill your canteen and put it in the freezer the night before, it will stay cool during the next day. (Be sure when you fill it to leave a little room for expansion as the water freezes.)

For more meals (an overnight trip for instance), or more substantial meals, you will need more than a pocket full of food, but a back pack offers plenty of room if you are able to do little compromising. Two things are important here: compact food and food that does not require refrigeration. Here are some foods that meet both criteria:

Meat: Commercially dried sausage, beef jerky, canned meat, chicken or fish.

Eggs: Dehydrated eggs.

Milk: Instant dry milk (use this instead of powdered "cream" in your coffee or tea too).

Butter: Margarine will keep a day or so in a small plastic container. You can also find it in tubes in some places.

Veggies: You'll probably have to forego your green leafies for the days that you are away, but dried fruit and canned vegetables can be taken along.

Other: Peanut butter in a small plastic container travels well as do all of the suggestions for pocket-foods. Water can be purified chemically or can be packed in. Small packets of dried flavor granules for soft drinks can add variety to beverages. Instant coffee, cocoa or tea bags. A few packaged pre-moistened towelettes.

INDISPENSABLE IDEA

In this day of exotic coffee makers, have you heard about boiled coffee? It's not for everyone but if you have been curious about it, here's how it's done. Use about one rounded tablespoon of fine-grind coffee for each cup. Put the coffee and the appropriate amount of cold water into a pot large enough to leave about three inches at the top so that the coffee won't boil over. Bring to a rolling boil and then remove the pot from the heat. Allow the coffee to settle and then return it to the heat once more. As soon as it starts to boil again, remove it from the heat and let it stand for a few minutes. Pour into cups and be prepared for a cup of strong, rich coffee.

You will undoubtedly have noticed that no mention has been made in this list of the great variety of foods available in pre-cooked, freeze-dried form. This is because they are products of a food processing industry that is developing very rapidly and the best way to decide what, if any, freeze-dried food to take is to go to your favorite sporting goods store and browse. You might want to take some samples home and try them out before taking them on the road. Although the quality of these foods is improving all the time, there are, of course, some that you will simply like better than others.

One final suggestion about backpacking is that you put all the ingredients for each meal in a separate self-locking plastic bag. This works well from several standpoints: you don't have to search through everyone's pack for the one item you need, you can pre-measure and pre-mix things and make sure that you have everything that is needed for each meal and, finally, you can use the plastic bag to carry off any refuse and trash that you may have after the meal.

WHEN YOU RENT A VACATION "HOME-AWAY-FROM-HOME"

A popular thing to do on a vacation is to rent a condominium, a cabin, a motor home, or boat. These accommodations are usually advertised as having a "fully-equipped kitchen" but clearly one person's idea of "fully-equipped" can be quite different from another's.

Even in the best possible circumstances you can almost certainly be sure that there will not be a sharp knife, the can opener will not work very well, the corkscrew is the kind guaranteed to tear holes in the cork instead of removing it, and there will not be a measuring cup.

As cook you can save yourself a lot of problems if you simply put together a box of things you personally consider essential in the kitchen and just take it along. If you duplicate things available in the "fully-equipped kitchen", nothing is lost but if you bring along just one "absolutely essential" item that is missing, it is worth the whole effort.

Some things you might want to have along would include:
a sharp paring knife
a good can opener
a reliable corkscrew
a measuring cup
a roll of paper towels
a hot pot holder
a flat grater
a jigger
a small cutting board
...and whatever else you are happy to have around when you cook while bearing in mind that part of a vacation is doing things a little differently than you do things at home.

THE PICNIC IN THE GREAT OUTDOORS

A picnic is a meal that you eat outdoors. How does that sound as a working definition? It has to be wide in concept because a picnic can be a simple back yard meal of fresh bread, cheese, and a bottle of wine ("A loaf of bread, a jug of wine and thou... "), an elaborate beach barbecue to celebrate being with friends in the heat of summer, a tailgate repast that turns your "getaway" car into a mobile buffet, or a quick break in a nearby green spot between morning and afternoon sessions at your office, or many, many other things.

Rather than discuss all the possibilities and permutations of the picnic, let's instead concentrate on the things that all picnics have in common.

First, you have to make sure that the food is going to be safe to eat. That sounds elementary and perhaps even a little insulting to the cook, but when food is going to be away from refrigeration for some time and will not be reheated before you and your party eat it, it is something to keep in mind. To ensure safe food, just remember to...

1. Choose your picnic menu at least partly based on the length of time it will be from the time you pack it until the time you eat it. If the time will be more than two hours and the food will not be refrigerated, avoid foods that contain dairy products (including foods like mayonnaise which contain raw eggs) and protein products. These foods are particularly susceptible to spoilage at warm temperatures.

2. Prepare your picnic foods as close to your departure time as possible, the less time bacteria have to multiply the better.

3. Wash your hands carefully before fixing picnic food. Use clean utensils and cutting boards. (Be sure not to cut fresh poultry or meat on a board and then use the same board to cut other foods that will be eaten without cooking, it is a very easy way to spread contamination.)

4. Foods to be eaten cold need to be thoroughly chilled before you leave home. Cold foods should be transported in a cooler but don't expect the cooler to "cool" the food, it has to be cold before you pack it to keep safely. When you arrive at the picnic site, keep the cooler closed until you are ready to eat. (You might consider

taking a separate cooler for drinks and snacks that you might want to have before mealtime.)

5.   Foods to be eaten hot should be completely heated before you leave home. Wide-mouth thermos containers are a good way to keep food hot while you are travelling to the picnic site. If you are serving a casserole or other large dish, prepare it for carrying by first wrapping in heavy-duty aluminum foil then in several (at least 8 or 10) layers of newspapers. Tie the whole package together or wrap it in a large towel.

You may want to cook at the picnic site and there are a number of small barbecues available that you can easily take. One thing to remember to take (in addition to matches and a bag of charcoal...) is a can of charcoal starter if you are using a charcoal barbecue. There are also small gas-fueled barbecues that are very quick to start and convenient to use but, alas, the result will lack that special grilled taste and the smoke-in-your-eyes authenticity of charcoal cooking.

Camp stoves are favored by some, particularly if you like breakfast picnics and want to cook eggs, bacon, and pancakes early in the morning for a ravenous crowd.

If you picnic a lot, you will undoubtedly find that you have stocked a picnic basket ready to go at all times. ("Have basket, will travel" as it were.) With a basket already pre-stocked with the utensils and accessories that you normally might need, all you have to add is food and you are on your way.

Some of the items to consider keeping in your pre-packed picnic basket might be:

      a reliable can opener
      a good corkscrew
      a utility knife
      a small cutting board
      whatever tableware you normally take
      a few plastic bags for disposing of trash
      plastic cups and/or glasses

salt and pepper
paper napkins
a picnic tablecloth (about 36x60 inches will take care of
　　most situations)
a small first-aid kit (including insect repellant)
a container of pre-moistened towelettes.

A carefully washed out gallon plastic milk container (or distilled water container) can serve double duty on a picnic. Fill it about two-thirds to three-fourths full with water and freeze it a day or two before your outing. Keep it with the picnic food and it will not only help keep the food cool and but also give you extra cold drinking water when you arrive at your destination.

When you plan your menu and pack, try to take only about the amount you and your party will eat. Picnic leftovers will not be fresh enough to eat later, and some foods are simply not safe for later eating.

Pack your picnic basket and cooler as you would a grocery bag with the heaviest items on the bottom and the items most susceptible to crushing on top.

There are a wide variety of containers with tight fitting lids available and they are perfect for salads, relishes, and other foods that might leak or spill. An extra wrap of aluminum foil adds protection and a little extra insulation too.

Picnics don't always have to be carefully planned... some you will remember with the most pleasure will be those that were strictly impromptu. A drive in the country and a stop at a small delicatessen or grocery to pick out some bread, cheese, cold cuts and fruit. The aroma of freshly baked bread coming out of a bakery on a warm spring day that makes you change your lunch plans from restaurant to park. Even a take-away lunch from your handy fast-food outlet eaten amidst trees and grass can qualify as a picnic... and what a change of pace it is from the normal lunch hour!

For reference, here are some of the pre-cut meats and cheeses you may expect to find at most delis:

DELICATESSEN MEATS

Roasted meats:

Beef: Usually quite lean, medium-well done and thinly sliced.

Corned beef: "Corned" (cured) in a spicy brine, this is saltier and spicier than straight roast beef, also usually has more fat.

Pastrami: Cured with a dry mixture of peppercorns and other spices and then smoked, it needs to have a little more fat than roast beef or corned beef in order not to seem too dry.

Ham: Thin slices of well trimmed ham with little fat (for special flavors try "country" hams which are cured with a variety of seasonings and smoked with smoke from different kinds of woods.)

Special hams:
"Country" hams come primarily from the southern and eastern parts of the US and differ from run-of-the-mill hams in the sort of food the pig was fed, the seasonings used, and the wood used to produce the smoke. These hams are more flavorful than "city" (standard commercially processed) hams that are usually available, they are also more expensive.

"Parma" hams from Italy (which include the famous Prosciutto ham) and Westphalian hams from Germany traditionally are dry-cured and air-dried, not smoked or cooked.

Smithfield hams are perhaps the most "gourmet" of gourmet American hams. Any ham labeled as a Smithfield Ham must be produced only in the small town of Smithfield, Virginia. The pigs used to make these wondrous hams are fed on local nuts of various kinds (acorns, peanuts, hickory nuts) and the hams are hickory-smoked.

Turkey breast: Usually quite large, but relatively thinly sliced, pieces

Turkey "Ham" and "Pastrami": These look-alikes are flavored to give the impression of ham and pastrami but without as many calories or as much cholesterol for those who need to be concerned with either or both.

Sausages of all kinds:

Bologna: All-time kids favorite (kids from a wide range of ages!), a mixture of beef, veal, and pork blandly seasoned.

Cervelat: A summer sausage of western European origin, more lightly seasoned than salami, usually not smoked, made of beef or pork or a combination of the two.

Mortadella: Closely related to bologna but prepared with more seasoning (notably garlic and peppercorns).

Pepperoni: Highly seasoned favorite from the pizza parlor but a tasty addition to any picnic.

Salami: There are a variety of salamis seasoned with different assortments of spices and herbs. Italian salamis are usually well-laced with garlic while salamis of German origin tend to omit it. You can choose salami made of beef (Kosher salami) or pork. Cotto salami is cooked while most other salamis are dried.

Thuringer: A smoked summer sausage of German origin, mildly seasoned usually a beef and pork combination.

Sliced pates and terrines are available at many delicatessens too. If you think of these somewhat exotic sounding meat dishes as simply well-seasoned meat loaf, you won't be too far afield.

A pate is a baked dish made up of ground meats usually including some sort of liver, well-seasoned with herbs, spices and often moistened with brandy.

A terrine in the current use of the term is basically the same thing although originally a pate was wrapped in a pastry case (hence "pate") while a terrine was encased in a layer of gelatin. Pates are sometimes served hot but strictly speaking, terrines are always served cold.

Some final thoughts about picnics...

Kids love picnics and love to help fix them too... a simple porch picnic on a rainy day can be an adventure in imagination if they are given a chance to decide on the menu and make up the sandwiches, cookies, and whatever else seems just right for the occasion.

Picnics are too much fun to limit just to certain situations: the park, the beach, and so forth. Try some unconventional picnics... If you live where winters are cold and long, how about an indoor Ground Hog Day picnic on February 2nd... just about the time you have forgotten how good cold fried chicken and potato salad can be, in time to remind you of all the warm spring and summer days that are just a few weeks away (even though there may be an icy blast if you opened the door). Or a midnight picnic after a movie or concert or evening sports event. Or a Sunday morning picnic brunch on your patio or balcony... let your imagination come up with some fun ways to enjoy unlikely situations and occasions.

Finally... THE BROWN BAG

Lots of us deal with the brown bag lunch every day and over the past several years manufacturers have come to recognize us as a good market for new ideas... all sorts of thermos containers, lunch boxes that can be pre-chilled, small lightweight containers, individually portioned foods... all of these things are a big help for the person who has to face THE BROWN BAG five days a week.

If you do prepare lunches-to-go on a regular basis, one thing that will make life a lot easier is a lunch preparation place. Set aside a drawer to hold plastic wrap and foil, paper bags, plastic containers, napkins, plastic utensils, spatulas for spreading and cutting, and anything else you find you use all the time. Have a cutting board stored nearby too. If possible, have your bread storage located right at hand. In other words, do all you can to save yourself extra steps around the kitchen while you are putting things together.

Here are some other ideas to solve lunch problems...

Soggy sandwiches are not welcomed by anyone and yet the things that make a sandwich really good are often the same things that will make it soggy when given half a chance. To avoid the soggies:

1. Make sure that the butter, margarine, mayonnaise, or peanut butter extends all the way out to the edge of the bread so that the oil from these spreads can insulate the bread from the moisture of the sandwich filling.

2. Make your own special flavored spreads by adding one of these to about a quarter cup of butter or margarine and mixing in well:

> 2 teaspoons of your favorite mustard
> 1 teaspoon of finely chopped onion and/or garlic
> 1 or 2 tablespoons of finely chopped parsley or chives
> 1/2 teaspoon (or to taste) of dried herbs such as basil, marjoram, oregano, or tarragon
> 1 or 2 tablespoons of freshly grated Parmesan cheese
> 1/2 teaspoon curry powder (or chili powder)
> or come up with your own special addition!

3. Wrap tomato slices, lettuce, sprouts, and such separately and add them to the sandwich just before it is eaten.

4. Cut two pieces of waxed paper somewhat larger than the slices of bread you are going to use. Put down the first slice of bread and add whatever spread you want then a piece of waxed paper, then the filling, another waxed paper sheet, and finally the last bread. When you are ready to eat, just pull the waxed paper sheets out, and cut the sandwich.

INDISPENSABLE IDEA

To soften butter in a hurry when you are making sandwiches, grate the amount you will need into a bowl and place the bowl over another bowl containing hot water.

The case against the frozen sandwich...

It is sometimes recommended that you simply make up a ton of sandwiches and put them in your freezer to be disinterred each day as needed. This is a recommendation that can only be made by someone who has not ever eaten a thawed sandwich.

In the first place you are quite limited in what can be frozen... no mayonnaise, no soft cheeses, no cooked egg whites, no cottage cheese, no fresh vegetables... the list is just about endless. In fairness, it should be noted that cooked meats and poultry, butter, peanut butter, and the bread itself freeze relatively well but that short list severely limits your lunch-bag creativity.

It's a better idea to just freeze the components for later use... keep a variety of breads in your freezer, slice or chop leftover chicken, turkey, or other meats and put in portion-sized containers that will thaw quickly. By doing this you can have a variety of fillings available on a moment's notice.

Everyone has their own favorite sandwiches but sometimes the person responsible for lunch-preparation needs an idea or two. To that end, here are some sandwich fillings that are good, inexpensive, and while not boring, not terribly exotic or cutsey either... most of us really would just as soon not face something in either of those categories for a mid-day meal.

Sliced meat (beef, pork, veal, corned beef, pastrami, tongue, etc.): vary the breads and the spreads, add sliced cheese and pack some greens separately. (To gather some new bread possibilities, check the chapter called Food Accessories later in this book.)

In addition to standard spreads of butter, margarine, and mayonnaise, you can add variation by using plain cream cheese or with cream cheese mixed with pickles, olives, mustard or mild horseradish added. (Incidentally, a very good spread can be made from mixing 1 part butter and 2 parts cream cheese together.

Spread sliced meats with a thin layer of coleslaw (that is not too moist).

With sliced pork roast add some apple butter.

Spread sliced corned beef with horseradish-seasoned mayonnaise.

Sliced meat loaf goes well with thousand island dressing.

Thinly sliced liver benefits from the flavor of crisp bacon pieces.

Meat salads are basically ground (or chopped) cooked meat mixed with mayonnaise or sour cream but the possible variations to this basic formula are extensive.

Ground lamb seasoned with curry powder and chutney

Ground lamb seasoned with fresh mint or mint jelly

Ground corned beef, grated cabbage, minced onion

Ground tongue, chopped mustard pickles

Ground pork roast, minced onion, salsa

Ground roast beef, mustard or horseradish mayonnaise

Ground roast beef, chopped sauteed onions and garlic

Crumbled cooked hamburger, corn niblets, minced onion, chili powder

Ground frankfurters mixed with baked beans and minced onion

Ground ham with a little drained crushed pineapple and seasoned with a dash of cloves

Ground ham, shredded cheese and chopped pickle

Tuna or other fish salad can be moistened with mayonnaise, dressing, sour cream, or yoghurt. To each three ounces of fish add one or more of the following...

a chopped or grated hard cooked egg

1 tsp. chopped capers

2 tbsp. chopped apple and 2 tbsp. chopped celery

1/4 cup well-drained small curd cottage cheese

3 tbsp. chopped celery, pickles, or green pepper

3 tbsp. grated swiss or provolone cheese

1/2 tsp. dried dill

Moisten egg salad as you would other salad fillings. For each three hard cooked eggs add one of these...

2 tbsp. crisp bacon bits

1/4 cup chopped canned corned beef

2 tbsp. each sliced ripe olives and chopped celery and 1/2 tsp. celery seed

1 tbsp. devilled ham

1/4 cup mixed chopped celery, green pepper and radishes

1/4 cup minced ham and 1 tbsp. mild mustard

1/2 tsp. curry powder (or to taste), 1 tbsp. grated onion

2 tbsp. chopped peanuts

Chicken or turkey salad can be varied by adding one of these to taste...

Hard cooked egg

Chopped ripe olive

Chopped celery and/or carrot

Finely chopped unpeeled apple and chopped celery

Chutney

Chopped peanuts

Peanut butter spread lightly on both sides of the bread with one of these between as a filling...

Grated carrots and raisins mixed with mayonnaise to blend

Crisp bacon bits

A mixture of chopped dried dates, apricots and/or figs

Chopped nuts mixed with creamed honey

Grated or thinly sliced cheese

Thin slices of ham

Crushed pineapple mixed with cream cheese

Cheese comes in so many varieties and all of them can be used either alone or combined with thin slices of meat, eggs, or vegetables.

Different mustards work well with sliced cheese too.

Or shred the cheese and mix it with chopped celery or pickle and mayonnaise to make a "cheese salad" sandwich.

Vegetarian sandwiches shouldn't be forgotten either...

Finely chopped cabbage, grated carrot and chopped nuts

Sprouts, grated carrot, chopped celery and green pepper

Finely chopped jicama, chopped peanuts, and grated carrot

Chopped radishes, cucumbers (cut out seed portion to keep the mix from being too moist), green peppers, finely chopped celery and sprouts

Or whatever you have on hand finely minced or grated and mixed with some tasty salad dressing. Make sure the final mixture will not be too moist. These fillings are often best packed separately and put onto the bread just before eating.

All of these sandwiches should be kept cool between packing and eating so if the person for whom the lunch is packed doesn't have a refrigerator available, look for lunch boxes that can be pre-chilled. Another way to keep food cool is to fill a small plastic storage container about three-fourths full of water and freeze it (or thoroughly chill small cans of juice). Add the container to the lunch box in the morning. There are also "blue-gel" coolers that are small enough to use in a lunch box or bag.

Fresh vegetables and fruits are great for take-alongs too. To make them easy to eat as finger food here are some suggestions...

Asparagus	Raw, tender stalks, cut in diagonal pieces
Broccoli	Use flowerets or peel the stalk and cut it into julienne pieces
Carrots	Carrot sticks of course
Cauliflower	Small flowerets
Celery	Sticks or chunks
Cucumber	Spears or slices (leave the peel intact sometimes, or take it off only partially)
Green pepper	Strips (red and yellow peppers sometimes too)
Jicama	Julienne strips or chunks
Sprouts	Good by themselves too
Tomatoes	Cherry tomatoes work best
Zucchini	Spears or slices

Other vegetables and salads require a small plastic container and spoon...

Beets	Pickled slices or cubes
Green beans	Marinated in a vinaigrette sauce
Dried beans	A variety of different kinds of cooked beans mixed together

	with a vinaigrette sauce to make a mixed bean salad
Corn	Corn relish or miniature corn ears
Olives	Ripe (black) or green
Pickles	The variety is endless...

Apples, bananas and oranges undoubtedly top the fruit hit-parade but give some others a chance to perform once in a while...

Apricots	Fresh in season, dried or canned
Berries	Fresh in season or frozen
Cantaloupe	Slice and wrap well in plastic or cut cubes or balls to go into a container
Cherries	In season or canned (home canned are less expensive than commercially canned, and better too)
Dates	Dried
Figs	Fresh or dried
Grapefruit	Half or sections well-wrapped in plastic
Mandarin oranges	Canned sections
Nectarines	In season or home canned since commercially canned are not easily available
Papaya	Wrap half well in plastic and slip in a wedge of lemon or lime
Peaches	In season or canned
Pears	Fresh (some variety is available almost all year round) or canned
Pineapple	Fresh spears or chunks or canned
Plums and Prunes	Fresh in season, canned or dried
Tangerines	Fresh in season

INDISPENSABLE IDEA

When you are going to freeze frosted cookies, frost them and then place them in the freezer on a tray for about 15 minutes to thoroughly set the frosting. Finally place in freezer containers and freeze. This way the frosting of one cookie will not stick to that of another.

One last thought about lunch packing... if a lunch box is used, be sure to wash it out after each use and occasionally give it a good scrubbing out with a baking soda and water solution to freshen it up. Containers used over and over for carrying lunches are bound to develop their communities of bacteria, and you don't want those communities to spread into your lunch.

Chapter 4:

WINE AND DINE

Oliver Wendell Holmes, while addressing the Massachusetts Medical Society in Boston on May 30, 1860, formally proclaimed:

"Wine is food."

Whether you agree with this particular weighty announcement or not, there is certainly little question that wine is a fine ingredient in, and superb companion for, food.

Wine has been around the human race for thousands of years. Imagine the surprise of the first person who tasted some juice from wild grapes that had "turned" and discovered it had in fact turned into something very special! That first vintner discovered what modern day vintners still know: wine making is a natural process that requires no special equipment, just time and natural ingredients.

If you have ever toured an American commercial winery and seen the enormous vats, tightly controlled environmental conditions, and highly mechanized bottling lines, you might doubt that wine making is a simple process, but it is. The only thing that all the controls and machinery do is insure consistent quality from bottle to bottle and from year to year.

WINE IN FOOD

Wine is used in cooked dishes in several ways: it is used as a liquid for poaching, it is used as a liquid in sauces, or it is used simply as a seasoning. As an ingredient, wine can add flavor, can tenderize meat, and can adjust the acidity of a dish.

The quality of wine used in cooking need not be great, but the liquid sold in supermarkets as "cooking wine" should be avoided at all costs-- you are better off using plain water!

Although you will sometimes find recommendations to use the same wine in preparing a dish that you plan to serve with the meal, there is no particular reason to do so. If you use something similar you will be quite satisfied--both reds, for instance, or both whites. When wine is used for poaching, the color of the wine should usually "match" the color of the food... white wines to poach fish for instance, reds with beef dishes.

When wine is used as a liquid ingredient in a sauce the same general rule applies as it does in poaching, usually you will match the color of the wine to the color of the sauce: white wines in light sauces, reds in dark sauces.

You will find recipes that call for champagne--the addition certainly sounds elegant, but in truth once heated, the champagne loses its bubbles and becomes just another still white wine. (Icy cold champagne over fresh strawberries or peaches is another matter of course!)

WHEN TO ADD WINE

The point at which you add wine to your dish will, of course, depend upon what you are preparing.

One point of clarification... once heated both the alcohol and the water content of wine evaporate. What remains is simply the flavor of the wine. If the wine is not cooked into the dish, however, the alcohol content remains.

Often a quickly sauteed dish would be enhanced with a sauce, typically the meat and/or vegetables are rapidly cooked over high heat and then removed to a warm platter while the sauce is prepared. Wine and other ingredients are added to the pan and briskly stirred to "deglaze" the pan and remove all of the succulent bits of food that have stuck to the sides and bottom. The sauce is boiled to reduce its volume and intensify the flavor and then poured with a flourish over the waiting meat.

In slow-cooked entrees, wine is best added no later than an 30 to 60 minutes before the dish will be completed (about the same time you add the final herbs). This half hour or so allows the alcohol and water in the wine to evaporate and the flavor of the wine to become part of the overall flavor of the finished dish.

On a longer time scale, wine is also used as an ingredient in marinades in which case it may be in contact with the meat for hours, or even days. The wine marinade can be used as a basting sauce too.

One small word of caution about using wine as an ingredient. This is definitely an area where you should not feel that if some is good, more would be better. It won't be. Wine can easily overcome other flavors to the detriment of the finished product. Be especially careful about adding wine (especially fortified wines such as sherry or port) to already prepared dishes such as soups or dessert sauces... taste as you go and stop just before you want to add "one last bit".

OTHER WAYS TO USE WINE IN COOKING

The uses of wine in cooking are just about infinite. A check through almost any recipe book will turn up scores of dishes from appetizers and soups through roasts and stews and on to puddings and cakes that call for wines of various kinds to complement the dish. What follows are some ideas that are not really recipes but may be the seed for some experimentation that will contribute to your reputation as a cook of excellence.

In soups:

>   Add about 1/4 cup of wine for each quart of clear soup.

>   Add about 1/4 cup medium sherry to each quart of heavy soups such as blackbean, lentil, or split pea.

In entrees:

> Add about 1/4 to 1/3 cup of red wine to liquid used for pot roast or other braised or stewed dishes.

> Use the same amount of white wine to braised light meats such as lamb, veal or pork.

> Use white wine in the poaching liquid for fish (equal parts of water and dry white wine).

> Use red table wine (preferably inexpensive) as a marinade for wildgame to remove some of the "strong" taste of the wild meat.

In desserts:

> Pour a small amount of port over peaches or pears.

> Add a sweet white wine (such as a sauterne or a rhine) to a fruit compote and chill.

> Pour champagne over strawberries served in a clear, stemmed glass.

> Add riesling to a combination of melon balls and garnish with the zest from an orange.

INDISPENSABLE IDEA

If you have a recipe that calls for dry white wine, it is sometimes possible to substitute dry vermouth by diluting the vermouth with an equal part of water. The herbs in the vermouth will affect the flavor of the dish, however, and you might want to experiment a bit to see if you find the results agreeable.

Another particularly useful way to use wines is as an "accent" and that is easily done by using a shaker bottle. These narrow-necked bottles filled with flavored wine can be a real asset in the kitchen.

Shaker bottles can be purchased but it is also possible to recycle bottles that have contained soy sauce or worcestershire sauce to use for this purpose. Carefully wash and remove labels from these bottles and fill with whatever mixture you like. To use as a shaker, simply put your thumb part-way over the opening and shake out the amount you need. Primitive, but effective. Start with the shakers about 3/4th filled with wine.

1. Dry sherry. Use it in chicken broth or beef consomme, and in such cream soups as cream of chicken, cream of mushroom, or seafood bisques.

2. Cream sherry. Use it to flavor custards and other puddings, shake on plain cakes (either butter or sponge cakes), shake a few drops into hot chocolate or coffee, shake onto fresh peaches or pears, add to whipped cream.

3. Flavored cream sherry. Add a drop or two of almond extract and use as suggested above.

4. Pepper sherry. Put 3-5 small dried red peppers into the shaker before adding a dry or medium sherry. It will take about a week to develop the flavor of the peppers and the longer the peppers steep, the hotter the sherry will become. Use in cajun dishes, in chili, and in stir-fried vegetables.

5. White table wine. Season with ingredients that go well with fish (lemon zest and/or juice, finely minced chives, parsley, or dill) and have the shaker available at the table to sprinkle on fish dishes.

6. Red table wine. Season with hearty seasonings such as oregano, thyme, or basil for several days. Use on meats and on green salads either as part of an oil-and-vinegar dressing or just by itself.

INDISPENSABLE IDEA

Here's something that will bring compliments from holiday dinner guests... use red wine for the liquid when making cranberry sauce from fresh cranberries. Both the flavor and the color will be enhanced.

WINE PRONUNCIATION GUIDE

Before we launch into a further discussion of wines, their uses, service, and affinities, here is a list, admittedly incomplete, of wines and wine-related words and an indication of the way they are commonly pronounced. The accented syllable is shown in all capital letters.

Alsace (Al-SASS), a French province bordering the Rhine, north of Switzerland famous for its white wines and often mentioned on the wine bottle label.

Amoroso (Ahm-oh-ROH-soh), a semi-sweet sherry, slightly less heavy than the Olorosos.

Amontillado (Ah-mone-tee-YAH-doe), a medium dry sherry, richer in flavor than the Finos but drier than the Olorosos.

Angelica (Ahn-ZHEL-i-cah), a sweet dessert wine of American origin.

Anjou (Ahn-SHOO), a French province on the Loire River particularly noted for its rose wines and often mentioned on wine bottle labels.

Aperitif (Ah-PARE-ee-teef), an appetizer wine (French).

Appellation Controlee (Ah-pell-AH-see-ahn cahn-trol-AY), when used on a label, it gives us the assurance that the wine in the bottle comes from the place named, the grapes named, and the approved methods of production for that area (French).

Asciutto (Ah-SHOOT-toe), dry (that is to say, not sweet) (Italian).

Asti (AHSS-tee), a town in the Piedmont area of Italy particularly famous for its sparkling wine, Asti Spumante.

Barbera (Bar-BARE-ah), red wine from Italy's Piedmont area.

Bardolino (Bar-doe-LEEN-o), light red wine from northern Italy.

Beaujolais (BOH-show-lay), red wine from France, also the name of the region of southern Burgundy (near Lyon) which produces the wine.

Blanc de blancs (Blahn duh Blahn), white wine made from white grapes (French). On a champagne label it means the same thing to differentiate it from standard champagne which is made from both white and black grapes.

Blanc de noirs (Blahn duh nwahr), white wine made from black (red) grapes (French). Blush wines are Blanc de noirs.

Bordeaux (Bor-DOE), area in southwestern France, the word, however, is used to describe a wide variety of red wines of greatly disparate quality.

Brut (Broot), very dry champagne (less sweet than extra-dry) (French).

Burgundy (BUHR-gun-dee), true Burgundy is a fine red wine from the French region southeast of Paris. It is also a word that has come, unfortunately, to mean red wine in general.

Cabernet (Kahb-air-NAY), excellent red wine grape (Cabernet Sauvignon) widely grown in Northern California as well as in the Bordeaux region of France, and also the wines produced from those grapes.

Campania (Kahm-PAHN-yah), district in Italy south of Rome which produces a large quantity of Italian table wines.

Campari (Kahm-PAR-ee), Italian aperitif.

Carafe (Kah-RAFF), decanter for serving wine at the table (sometimes you will see the French version of the word, carafe (Kahr-ah-FAY) used.

Chablis (SHAHB-lee), a popular white wine from California, originally from an area in France southeast of Paris, Chablis wines are normally made of Chardonnay grapes.

Champagne (Sham-pane), specifically sparkling white wine produced in, and made from the grapes grown in, the Champagne region of France. Other white sparkling wines may use the word "champagne" with the place of their origin, for instance "California Champagne". Generically the word is used to describe any white sparkling wine.

Chardonnay (SHAR-doe-nay), fine white wine grape, in the United States it is usually called Pinot Chardonnay although botanically the grape has no relationship to the other Pinots.

Chateau (Sha-TOH), country estate (French).

Chateauneuf-du-Pape (Shah-toh-NUFF dooh Pahp), red wine from the Rhone valley, its name comes from the fact that it was the "new" (neuf) "country estate" (chateau) of the Avignon Popes in the fourteenth century. The wine is a blend of grapes grown in the region

Chenin blanc (SHAY-nahn blahn), excellent and popular white wine grape growth both in the United States and in France.

Chianti (Kee-AHN-tee), Italian red table wine, inexpensive and often sold in a raffia-wrapped bottle. Chianti Classico is a better wine sold in normal wine bottles and usually aged.

Claret (KLAHR-et), generic name used mainly in England to describe red table wine of unknown origin.

Cold Duck, this blend of a still white wine and a sparkling red is mainly interesting because of the derivation of its name which centers around what was probably a typesetting error. The German name for the blend is Kalte Ende (cold end or conclusion), but some careless typesetter changed the final "d" to a "t" and it became Kalte Ente which translates as "cold duck".

Colombard (KOH-lahm-bahr), white wine grape grown both in France and the United States, often used in blended white wines both still and sparkling.

Demi-sec (Dehmi Sehk), a somewhat sweet champagne.

Doux (Doo), the word means "sweet" in French and is applied to some wines to indicate sweetness in lieu of flavor. Doux champagne is the sweetest of the champagnes.

Dubonnet (Dooh-buhn-AY), a sweet, red fortified French aperitif.

Eiswein (ICE-vine), wine made from the first pressing of frozen grapes (German).

Est! Est! Est! (just the way it looks)... cannot be passed without telling the story behind the name of this light white Italian wine. The tale goes that a certain wine-loving German bishop was making a trip to Rome and sent a runner on ahead to find the inns that had the best wine. When the runner found such a place he was to write "Est!" (Latin for

"It is") on the wall of the inn. When the runner reached Montefiascone, a small village just north of Rome, the wine was so good he wrote Est! Est! Est! on the wall. The bishop enjoyed the wine so much that he over-indulged himself and died in Montefiascone, probably drunk and happy. The inscription on his tomb there commemorates the event.

Fino (FEE-noe), a very pale and very dry sherry.

Folle Blanche (Fall Blahnch), a white wine grape of France and also grown in the United States and used in blended white wines and some white sparkling wines.

Fortified, not pronunciation but a bit of an explanation of this term which is used to describe both aperitif and dessert wines. It means that something has been added to the natural wine to increase its alcohol content.

Frascati (Frahs-KAHT-ee), a dry golden Italian table wine.

Freisa (FRAY-eessa), an Italian red wine grape.

Fume-blanc (Few-MAY blahn), wine made from sauvignon blanc grapes.

Gamay (Ga-MAY), an excellent red wine grape from the Beaujolais area in France, also used to make a rose.

Gewurztraminer (Geh-VERTZ-trah-meen-ehr), white wine grape from Germany which is also grown in the United States and produces a slightly spicy wine.

Graves (Grahv), area in France near Bordeaux, the word describes the soil there, "gravel". The region produces both red and white wines.

Grenache (Greh-NAHSH), a good wine grape used to make a popular and excellent rose wine and also used in blended red wines.

Grignolino (Grin-yoh-LEE-no), Italian red wine grape and the wine made from it.

Groslot (Groh-LOH), Red wine grape originating in the Loire valley of France, used in blends particularly roses.

Haut (Oh), a French word that means "high", relating to wines it usually is part of a place name such as Haut-Medoc (Oh May-dahk) which is the upland portion of the Medoc area of France.

Hock, a name commonly used in Britain to describe Rhine wines. The name probably taken from the German village of

Hochheim (HOCK-hime). Hock wines are usually sold in brown bottles.

Jug wine, is a phrase used to describe inexpensive blended wines sold in half-gallon or gallon bottles. Often produced by well known wineries these are the American equivalent of the French vin ordinaire, the Italian vino de tavola, Spanish vino corriente, and German Tishwein.

Kokinelli, a resin-flavored red wine from Greece, see Retsina for more details about resinated wines.

Lachryma Christi (LAH-cree-mah KRIS-tee), a white wine from the slopes above Naples, Italy... there are a number of stories about the derivation of the name, which translates literally as "tears of Christ".

Lambrusco (Lahm-BROOS-koh), an almost-sparkling wine from northern Italy.

Liebfraumilch (LEEB-frau-milsch), a sweetish white wine of varying quality since the name has become used so widely. Probably originated from the vineyards of the Liebfrauenkirche (Church of the Blessed Mother) in Worms, Germany. The name literally translates to Milk of the Blessed Mother.

Lillet (LEE-lay), a light dry French fortified aperitif.

Madeira (Meh-DEER-eh), a fortified wine originating in the Portuguese island of Madeira.

Malaga (MAHL-ah-gah), Spanish fortified wine.

Manzanilla (Mahn-thahn-NEEL-yah), the palest and driest of all Spanish sherries.

Marsala (Mahr-SAHL-ah), Italian fortified wine.

Mateus (Mah-TIOOS), a popular slightly sweet rose table wine from Portugal.

May wine, a wine punch originating in Germany. The wine is sweetened and steeped with fresh woodruff. In celebration of spring the punch bowl and cups can be decorated with early fresh strawberries.

Merlot (Mair-LOH), a fine red wine grape which is made into its own wine called by the same name and also used in blended red wines.

Molinara (Moh-lee-NAHR-ah), an excellent Italian red wine grape blended into Valpolicella and Bardolino wines.

Moscato (Mohs-CAH-toh), the Italian muscat grape which turns up in many Italian wines of varying quality.

Moselle (Moh-ZELL in French pronunciation, MOH-z'l in German), a wine growing district that follows the Moselle River through France, Luxembourg, and Germany, this northerly area produces a delicate white wine.

Muscadet (Muhs-kahd-AY), a light French wine.

Muscat (MUHS-kaht), a sweet grape used in wine, and also eaten fresh and used to produce raisins. Muscat is also the name of a sweet fortified wine.

Neuchatel (NUH-shah-tel), a white wine from Switzerland.

Oenology (EE-noh-loh-gee), the study of wines and winemaking.

Oloroso (Oh-loh-ROH-soh), a medium to dark sherry, heavier than the Amontillados with a rich aroma.

Petit Syrah (Peh-TEE SEE-rah), a wine grape grown in California probably from stock from the Rhone Valley in France, the California production is often used in blended red table wines.

Pinot (PEE-noh), a family of the highest quality wine grapes which includes Pinot Noir (Nwahr), Pinot Blanc (Blahn), Pinot Gris (Gree).

Port, a sweet wine from originating in Portugal which is available in several varieties (ruby, tawny, and others). Vintage Port is made from the wines of the harvest year specified on the label. Port wines produced outside of Portugal must specify the place of origin on the label (such as California Port).

Pouilly Fuisse (POO-yee FWEE-say), excellent dry white table wine from southern Burgundy in France.

Pouilly Fume (POO-yee Few-MAY), white table wine, not as dry as Pouilly Fuisse.

Recioto (Ray-CHIOH-toh), a sweet red wine from the Valpolicella area of Italy.

Retsina (REHT-sin-ah), a white wine from Greece which is flavored with resin. In ancient times the Greeks stored their wines in pottery containers called amphorae. To prevent evaporation they coated the inside of the jars with resin which, not surprisingly, flavored the wine. Whether the Greeks liked the wine in spite of the taste or because of it, we will never know but the flavor of resin permeates some (not all) Greek wines to this day. Resinated red wine is called Kokinelli.

Riesling (REESS-ling), a very old, very famous wine grape from the Rhine valley now grown in many parts of the world. Many wines called "riesling" are, however not of this superior quality. In most cases a Johannesburg Riesling denotes a higher quality wine than just the term Riesling on the label.

Rioja (Ree-OH-hah), an important wine growing district in Spain.

Rose (Roh-ZAY), the French word for pink. Roses are not a combination of white and red wine, but are a special way of fermenting grapes that would normally produce red wine. Roses ferment for a while with the grape skins left in the mixture, then the skins are removed for the remainder of the fermentation time.

Rosso (ROSS-oh), the Italian word for red and frequently seen as vino rosso (VEE-noh ROSS-oh) which means red wine... any red wine made anywhere by anybody.

Sake (Sah-keh), a Japanese alcoholic beverage that is popularly called a wine but really isn't. It is brewed from fermented rice and is an excellent accompaniment to Japanese food, as you might expect. Sake is served at about 90 degrees Fahrenheit and traditionally poured from a small, porcelain vase-like server into tiny cups.

Sangria (Sahn-GREE-ah), a cold wine punch, popular in the summer.

Sauterne or Sauternes (Soh-TERN), a fine, sweet, golden wine from France which originated in the town of Sauternes. The name of the town gives the wine its name in French and that is why when speaking of the French wine the word always ends with an "s" whether you are speaking of one or several. The American version of the wine is called "sauterne" without the final "s").

Sauvignon or Sauvignon Blanc (SOH-veen-yahwn), very fine quality white wine grape and the wine made from it, also used in some blended white wines.

Schaumwein (SHOHM-vine), German word for sparkling wine.

Sec (Sehk), a French word that means dry, when used to describe champagne, however, it is less dry (sweeter) than Brut.

Semillon (SAY-mee-yahwn), white wine grape often used in blended white wines.

Soave (SWAH-vay), Italian dry white wine.

Solera (Soh-LEHR-ah), method for making sherry whereby more mature vintages are mixed with younger vintages in a sequential way so that the final sherry is a blend of the harvests from any years. This is why there is no such thing as a vintage year on a sherry bottle.

Spatlese (SHPATE-lay-zeh, used in German wine making to designate late harvest grapes, usually very ripe and sweeter than the same grapes picked earlier in the season (German).

Spumante (Spoo-MAHN-tay), Italian word for sparkling or foamy.

Sylvaner (Sill-VAHN-er), German white wine grape, grown in the United States and sometimes blended into American rieslings.

Syrah (See-RAH), red wine grape.

Tinta (TEEN-tah), Portuguese red wine grape varieties.

Tipico (TEE-pee-coh), the Italian equivalent of the French phrase "Appellation Controlee".

Tishwein (TISH-wine), German table wine (similar to French vin ordinaire)

Tokay (Toh-KAY), true Tokay wines are fine white wines from northeastern Hungary.

Traminer (Tram-MEE-ner), a white wine grape grown in Germany, France, and the United States

Valpolicella (Vahl-poh-lee-CHEL-ah), an excellent and versatile red Italian table wine.

Vermouth (Ver-MOOTH), a pair of fortified and herb-flavored wines. White vermouth is frequently called French vermouth and is used as an appetizer wine, while red vermouth is frequently called Italian vermouth and often served as a dessert wine.

Vin (Van), French word for wine.

Vin ordinaire (Van ohr-deen-air), a phrase that can be applied to white, red, or rose wines and simply indicates that it is a wine of no particular area or variety of grapes. Vin ordinaire is what most of us drink most of the time... quite happily.

Vinho verde (VEEN-hoh VAIR-day), a wine from Portugal, literally translated means "green wine" but the "green" refers to its age (young), not its color.

Vino corriente (VEE-noh Cohr-ee-EHN-tay), Spanish table wine similar to vin ordinaire.

Vino da tavola (VEEN-oh dah TAH-voh-lah), Italian table wine similar to vin ordinaire.

Viticulture, the science of grape growing.

Vintage, the annual grape harvest of a specified region and, consequently, the wine made from those grapes.

Vouvray (Voo-VRAY), white wine from the Loire valley.

Zinfandel (ZIN-fahn-del), a popular red wine grape heavily produced in the western United States and used in varietal wine, blanc de noir, and blended wines.

FOOD AND WINE NATURAL AFFINITIES

Because of the levels of acidity and tannin, and because of the unique flavor that each wine has, there are certain combinations of wine and food that seem to work especially well. This list makes note of some of them but these are suggestions only and should not be taken as law. Everyone has their own sense of what "tastes right". Some of these suggestions may not seem agreeable to your particular sense of taste while other combinations not shown here seem just perfect. After you have done some tasting and comparing, make your own judgments.

APPETIZER WINES (APERITIFS)

Appetizer wines are served before meals or by themselves with some light snacks. These wines go well with typical appetizers such as the nuts, hors d'oeuvres, crackers and spreads that we often serve before a meal or to guests who drop in for a casual get-together.

SPECIFIC APPETIZER WINES
Madeira
Sherries:
    Manzanilla (extremely dry)
    Fino (dry)

Dry or Cocktail sherry
Amontillado (semi-dry)
Amoroso (semi-sweet)
Golden sherry (medium sweet)
Oloroso (heavy flavor)
Cream sherry: See Dessert Wines
Vermouth, White (French)
Vermouth, Red (Italian): See Dessert Wines

Champagne is also an excellent aperitif, as are the many herb and fruit flavored brand named appetizer wines such as Dubonnet, Lillet, Campari and many others.

WHITE TABLE WINES

In general white table wines are best with lightly flavored entrees: fish, seafood, chicken, turkey, egg-based dishes, pork, and veal. When served with heavier, richer dishes their more delicate flavor tends to be smothered.

SPECIFIC WHITE WINES
Chablis, also particularly good with lamb
Chardonnay, also goes well with rich main dishes such as lobster or salmon
Chenin Blanc, especially good with pork, also good with ham and sweet-sour dishes
Emerald Riesling, similar to White Riesling
Est! Est! Est!
Folle Blanche
Frascati
French Colombard
Fume Blanc, See Sauvignon Blanc
Gewurztraminer, also good with ham, mild sausage and curried foods, can be used as an appetizer wine
Graves, goes well with turkey
Green Hungarian, also goes well with pork

Grey Riesling
Hock, A British general terms for Rhine,
    See Rhine Wine
Johannesburg Riesling, particularly nice
    with mild fish and crab dishes
Moselle, See Rhine
Muscat Canelli, best with dishes contain-
    ing fruits, or pleasant just to sip
Pinot Blanc
Pouilly Fuisse, good with turkey
Rhine Wine, slightly sweet and par-
    ticularly good with fruit and to
    take on picnics or for sipping
Riesling
Sauterne/Sauternes
Sauvignon Blanc, particularly good with
    oysters
Semillon, good with scallops
Soave
Sylvaner
Traminer
White Riesling, varies but can be quite
    sweet
White Zinfandel, good with ham and
    mild sausage

RED TABLE WINES

In general red table wines are best with beef and other red meats (steaks, roasts, chops, organ meats), wild game and birds, entrees with spice tomato-based sauces, pasta dishes and cheese dishes. These wines have a heavier, heartier flavor than the lighter, more delicate whites.

SPECIFIC RED WINES

Barbera, particularly good with spicy
    foods
Bardolino
Beaujolais, good with turkey
Bordeaux, also good with turkey
Burgundy

Cabernet Sauvignon, particularly good
    with lamb, duck, and barbecued
    meats
Chianti, the traditional accompaniment
    for Italian foods made with
    tomato-based sauces
Claret
Gamay
Gamay Beaujolais
Grenache (also used to make rose wine)
Grignolino
Merlot, particularly good with lamb,
    duck, game birds and barbecued
    meat; also good with salmon
Petit Syrah (or Sirah)
Pinot Noir
Ruby Cabernet
Valpolicella
Zinfandel

ROSE AND BLUSH WINES

These light wines may be served with any kind of food but are perhaps most compatible with the more flavorful light dishes (shrimp, oysters, lobster, halibut, red snapper, trout, spicier turkey, chicken dishes and curries) and the milder of the red meats (pork, lamb, veal). These wines are also nice for picnics and can be used as appetizer wines. They can range from quite dry to a little sweet.

SPECIFIC ROSE WINES

Gamay
Grenache
Tavel

You will also see "Blush" wines, sometimes called "Blanc de Noirs", for sale. They may be served as you would serve any of the traditional rose wines.

SPARKLING WINES

These festive wines may be served with any kind of food under virtually any circumstances. They may also be served alone or in conjunction with other drinks at a cocktail party and are elegant additions to any picnic.

SPECIFIC SPARKLING WINES

Asti Spumante
Champagnes
> Vintage (very dry), an exceptional wine for special occasions
> Natural (very dry), particularly good with rich cheese
> Brut (dry), particularly good as an appetizer
> Extra Dry or Extra Sec (semi-sweet), particularly good as an addition to party punches
> Sec (medium sweet)
> Demi-Sec (rather sweet)
> Doux (very sweet)
Crackling Wines (not as effervescent as champagne)
Pink Champagne (a sparkling version of rose wine)
Sparkling Burgundy (a sparkling red)

DESSERT WINES

In general these sweet wines are served either at the end of the meal or simply for sipping. They taste right with fruits, semi-sweet dry cookies, nuts, and dessert cheeses.

SPECIFIC DESSERT WINES

Angelica
Cream Sherry, noted above
Late Harvest Riesling, good with vanilla custards
Malaga
Madeira
Marsala
Muscat, particularly good with nuts
Port particularly good with cheeses and nuts
> Ruby (red, rich, and fruity)

Tawny (well aged, mellow and subtle)
White (driest port)
Vintage (aged in the bottle rather than in the
    cask)
Sauterne/Sauternes
Tokay

SERVING TEMPERATURES FOR WINES

Wine flavor is affected by the serving temperature of the wine. White wines served too warm seem dull and flat, while most red wines when served chilled lose their richness of flavor. Experiment for yourself and see that this is not just wine-fancier's lore, but is a perceivable fact.

No matter what the temperature of the room, no wine should be served that is at more than 70 degrees Fahrenheit.

Appetizer wines:	Most flavorful when served at room temperature but some prefer the wines slightly cooled.
White table wines:	Typically served at about 55 degrees Fahrenheit. A bottle of wine stored at room temperature will reach 55 degrees after about one hour in the refrigerator. Serving the wine colder will accentuate tartness and diminish the apparent sweetness.
	A very dry white may be served at nearer to room temperature to mellow the flavor. (Low tannin red wines can also benefit from slight cooling. This would include such wines as Bardolino and Valpolicella from Italy.)
Red table wines:	Red wines are traditionally served at room temperature (65 to 70 degrees Fahrenheit). Cooling a red wine will heighten the perception of tannin and make the wine seem more tart. (Remember rooms are warmer during

the summer months and you will want to
cool the reds just a bit before serving.)

Rose and blush wines: Normally served slightly cooled, at about the
same temperature as whites.

Sparkling wines: Served quite chilled, about 45 degrees
Fahrenheit. By serving the wine at a cooler
temperature it keeps its bubbles longer.

Dessert wines: Best when served at room temperature.

PREPARING A WINE TO BE SERVED

STILL WINES

All non-sparkling table wines and many appetizer and dessert wines
require a tool to remove the cork. Several varieties are available but
probably the most reliable is some variant on the traditional corkscrew.

Opening the bottle.
Cut through the foil covering the top of the bottle with a sharp knife
just below the lip of the bottle.

Remove the foil to the point where you have made the cut. Wipe the
now exposed cork and the top of the bottle clean. This step is less important in bulk produced American wines, but essential when the wine
has been aged for some time.

Insert the corkscrew into the center of the cork and turn in as far
as you can then, very gently, ease the cork out with as little disturbance
as possible to the wine itself. Again this precaution is more important
in aged wines where sediment may have accumulated in the bottle.

Wipe the mouth of the bottle after the cork has been removed.

Decanting a still wine.
There are really two reasons for this process.

First, if the wine is a "jug wine", it will be much easier to serve if it is poured into smaller, more easily handled container.

Second, is the traditional reason: by pouring the wine from its original bottle into another container the sediments can be left in the original bottle. These sediments are mainly crystals of tartrates and coloring matter and are tasteless as well as harmless, but also do not add anything to the pleasure of drinking the wine and so are best left behind.

Here is the traditional way to decant a bottle of wine. Place a candle next to the decanter with the flame at about the height of its top. Pour the wine from the original bottle slowly past the flame into the decanter and stop pouring as soon as the first sediment can be seen in the stream of liquid.

SPARKLING WINES

Dramatic as it may be to "pop the cork" of a champagne bottle it is both safer for you and better for the wine to open the bottle more gently.

Point the cork of the chilled bottle away from everyone. Hold the cork in place by cradling the top of the neck in your hand while you remove the wires and paper. Keep firm pressure on the cork while, with the other hand, twisting the bottle slightly until the cork begins to turn. Gently work the cork out of the bottle while keeping the bottle pointed up at an angle of about 45 degrees from vertical. Having a cloth napkin handy is a good idea, as is having your champagne glasses nearby because when the cork comes out the champagne is ready to pour immediately.

INDISPENSABLE IDEA

If you are serving champagne...

Chill the bottle only up the point where it curves into the neck and the cork will be easier to remove.

If the bottle has a plastic cork that is recalcitrant, briefly run hot water on the top of the neck of the bottle. The warmed glass will expand and the cork will come out more easily.

Chill the champagne only until the bottle feels cool. Don't leave it in the refrigerator for a long time before serving.

WHY "RED WINE WITH MEAT, WHITE WINE WITH FISH"?

Several reasons... first this pairs the heavier, more full-bodied red wines with the dark and strongly flavored meats and the lighter, more delicately flavored white wines with poultry, seafood, and lighter meats such as port. There are certainly workable exceptions to this rule but it is a classic, traditional, and reasonable pattern to follow. An additional reason for the pairing has to do with the presence or absence of tannin in the wine. Red wines are fermented with the wine skins which add this chemical to the liquid. Tannin cuts through the "fattiness" of red meat and makes it more digestible. It also is a factor in the longevity of the wine (and the reason the red wines age well while white wines are usually consumed while they are "young").

WINE SWEETNESS

In general it is important to pair wines with food in a broad matching of sweetness level. If the sweetness of one is much greater than the sweetness of the other, it will intensify the perceived "sourness" of the less-sweet partner.

Late harvest grapes have the highest sugar level and are the ones used to produced a naturally sweet wine. These very sweet wines are served at the end of a meal.

Terms used to describe the sweetness of wine are not particularly meaningful on their own, but there is an accepted standard behind them:

> A wine classified as "dry"
> has less than 1.0 percent residual sugar.
> A wine classified as "semi-dry"
> has less than 1.5 percent residual sugar.
> A wine classified as "medium dry"
> has from 1.5 to 2.5 percent residual sugar.
> A wine classified as "sweet"
> has more than 2.5 percent residual sugar.
> A sherry classified as "dry"
> has less than 2.5 percent residual sugar.
> A sherry classified as "medium"
> has 2.5 to 4 percent residual sugar.

WINE AND CHEESE MATCH-UPS

Wine and cheese are born companions and, in the manner of good friends, bring out the best in each other. Some combinations are so perfectly balanced that they have become classic--Port with Stilton, Cabernet Sauvignon and Camembert for instance. But other combinations, if not quite so classic, are excellent either on their own or as a course to end the meal in a leisurely way... and an excuse to linger at the table after a good meal.

With wine and cheese serve either crackers or pieces of unbuttered bread. If crackers are served, unsalted ones are best because the cheese is already well-salted. As an end-of-meal course, fruit is a nice accompaniment... some grapes, ripe pears or peaches for instance.

Using the same descriptive designations for the various types of cheeses that are found in THE COOK'S BOOK OF ESSENTIAL INFORMATION, here are some combinations that most people will find agreeable:

These Varieties of Cheese	Go with These Wines
Soft Unripened cheeses: Cream cheese, Neufchatel, Crema Dania, Corolle	Dry whites or champagne: Fume Blanc, Johannesburg Riesling, Chardonnay Colombard, Chenin Blanc
Firm Unripened cheeses: Mozzarella, Mysost, Gjetost	Light Reds: Valpolicella, Beaujolais
Soft Ripened cheeses: Brie, Camembert, Limburger Liederkranz, Teleme	Rich, mature reds: Cabernet Sauvignon, Pinot Noir (also Pinot Blanc), Merlot
Semisoft Ripened cheese: Port Salut, Bel Paese, Saint- Paulin, Tourton, Fontina	Fruity reds and whites: Beaujolais, Gamay, Chenin Blanc, Valpolicella
Tilsit, American Brick, Beer Cheese (Bierkase)	Full-bodied reds: Petit Sirah, Zinfandel (good with beer too)
Firm Ripened cheeses: Cheddars, Cheshire, Double Glouster, Colby, Longhorn	Mellow mature reds: Gamay, Beaujolais, "Burgundy" jug wine (good with beer too)
Firm Ripened cheeses: Gouda, Havarti, Muenster, Edam, Provolone	Light reds: Beaujolais, Merlot, Ruby Cabernet, Valpolicella
Firm Ripened Swiss type cheese: Emmental, Gruyere, Jarslberg, Samsoe, Blarney, Appenzeller	Fruity reds and whites: Beaujolais, Barbera, Gamay, Zinfandel

WINE AND DINE

Very Hard Ripened cheeses:
  Parmesan, Grana, Asiago,
  Romano

Full-bodied reds:
  Bardolino, Barbera,
  Zinfandel, Chianti

Blue-veined Mold Ripened cheeses:
  Blue, Gorgonzola, Roquefort,
  Stilton

Full-bodied reds:
  Barbera, Petit Sirah, Pinot
  Noir, Cabernet Sauvignon

Goat cheeses:
  Feta, Chevres

Dry, fruity reds and whites:
  Retsina, Chardonnay,
  Sauvignon Blanc, Cabernet
  Sauvignon, Ruby Port

WHICH WINE IS BEST?

There is no "right" answer to this question.

The Romans understood the problem very well and summed it up in one of their sayings: *"De gustibus non disputandum"* (roughly translated the phrase means that there is simply no accounting for taste).

You should be comfortable drinking and serving what you like, not what some wine "expert" tells you that you ought to like. The best course is to be open-minded and experiment. Try different types of wine and different vintners... try wines from Italy and Hungary and Australia... try wines from California and Washington state and Ohio. Give your taste buds a chance to see what is out there before you make any final decisions about what you like. Be prepared to see your preferences change however.

Most people start out by preferring a sweet light wine and some will continue to prefer that kind of wine. Others find that their taste subtly shifts toward drier wines usually dry whites first and later the dry rich reds.

But... let your taste and preference be your guide and remember that you are never "wrong" in your choice. There are some who drink red wine with everything and others who would never drink anything but white. Neither is wrong... they are just exercising their absolute right to choose what they like.

If you are going to provide a bottle or two as a hospitality gift when dining at a friend's home, you are always safe in taking a rose or blush. If you know what the entree is to be, you can select something perhaps more to the point, but a rose is always safe. Another safe choice is champagne, and California champagnes (or sparkling whites) are about the same price as a reasonably good still wine.

INDISPENSABLE IDEA

When serving wine at the table you can avoid wine drips on your tablecloth if, when the wine has been poured, you twist the bottle to the right (or to the left if you are left-handed) as you lift it to the upright position. Those potential stains run right back into the bottle.

WINE GLASSES

Wine is something that appeals to all of the senses... sight as much as any other. The rich reds and pale yellows of the wines reveal themselves beautifully in a clear glass. The traditional stemmed glass accomplishes two functions: it allows the wine to be held without absorbing warmth from the hand, particularly important in wines that are served cooled, and it gives the wine more visual importance at the table.

Any kitchenware shop, department store, jewelry shop, or discount store has a variety of glasses to choose among from the very versatile all-purpose wine glass which has a capacity of about seven ounces, to special purpose glasses for sherries, reds, whites, and champagne.

Prices vary from modest to expensive, just remember that what the glasses hold is more important than the glasses themselves.

Wine should never be poured to completely fill a glass. Always leave about a third of the glass unfilled so that the wine can aerate and the aroma can develop.

Appetizer wines are served in small wine or cocktail glasses that hold two to three ounces. Traditionally sherry can be served in special deep, narrow glasses that hold about three ounces.

Red and white table wines can be served either in the all-purpose glass or in glasses designed for them.

Sparkling wines are most often served either in the wide and shallow champagne saucer with solid or hollow stem, or in a champagne flute which has a narrow tall glass bowl. The flute retains the effervescence longest, while champagne saucers or hollow-stemmed glasses allow the bubbles to escape quickly. Each holds about 4 ounces.

CLASSIC ORDER OF SERVING WINE WITH FORMAL MEALS:

With appetizer course: Chablis or Champagne (Natural or Brut)
With soup course: Dry Sherry or Madeira
With fish course: Dry white wine
With entree course: Light red wine
With meat course: Full-bodied red wine
With dessert course: Sauterne or Champagne (Extra dry)
With cheese course: Port or Cream Sherry

WINE SERVINGS PER BOTTLE SIZE

When planning wine purchases it is useful to know about how much will be needed.

	6 oz. servings (table wines)	3 oz. servings (dessert wines)
375 milliliters (split) (approximately 1 1/2 cups)	2	4
750 milliliters (fifth) (approximately 3 cups)	4	8
1 liter (approximately 4 cups)	5-6	11

	6 oz. servings (table wines)	3 oz. servings (dessert wines)
1 1/2 liters (approx. 6 cups) (approximately 6 cups)	8	16
3 liters (approximately 12 cups)	16	32

A useful formula for estimating how much wine to buy is this... allow about a half of a 750ml ("fifth") bottle for each person if the meal is substantial, less if the meal is light. People who are accustomed to drinking wine regularly with their meals will probably drink more than this amount, those who do not drink wine regularly will probably drink less.

Incidentally you should always be prepared for those among your guests who do not drink wines for health, dietary, religious, or personal preference reasons. There are nonalcoholic wines available at most supermarkets and health food stores that handle this situation easily. Juice or sparkling water are other possible substitutions.

INDISPENSABLE IDEAS

If you are calorie conscious, or have dieters as guests, consider wine coolers or spritzers... half wine and half club soda in a regular sized wine glass cuts the calories by fifty percent but gives a full glass of something pleasant to drink.

THE LABEL ON THE BOTTLE

A careful reading of the label on a bottle of wine can provide a surprising amount of information. Some of the information is required Federal and state law and some is voluntary, some is unabashedly promotional.

Required information includes brand, type of wine, the place of origin, the bottler's name and location, and the alcohol content.

The type of wine is the generic, varietal, or proprietary designation assigned to it by the wine maker. Burgundy, for instance has become a generic type of wine, while Cabernet Sauvignon is a varietal. Wineries often select a name to be used with specific blendings, particularly of table wines... such names as Mountain Burgundy, for instance, have no particular meaning beyond saying that it is a red table wine.

Place of origin has some specific requirements. For instance, to use the word "California" on the label, it is required that all of the grapes must come from that state. To use a county name 75 percent must come from within the county limits. To use an Approved Viticulture Area designation (such as Napa Valley) 85 percent of the grapes must come from that Area.

The bottler of the wine is often different from the winery that produced it. On imported wines, the name of the importer and distributor are also noted.

Finally, the label must indicate the alcohol content of the wine. The legal range for table wine is from 7 to 13.9 percent. Sparkling wines range from 10 to 13.9 percent. The alcohol content of appetizer and dessert wines can be no higher than 20 percent

Voluntary information includes vintage (95 percent of the grapes must be from the harvest year stated on the label), descriptive characteristics (this information may range from specific residual sugar content to quite subjective descriptive terms), and name of individual vineyard (95 percent of the grapes have to have come from the named vineyard).

WINE STORAGE

Corked bottles should be stored horizontally which allows the cork to stay moist and consequently airtight in the bottle. Bottles with screw-on caps are best stored upright. The more alcohol in the wine, the better it stores. Sherries and other fortified wines, for instance, can be stored in their original bottles or decanters for long periods of time.

Wines keep best in a temperature range from 55 to 60 degrees Fahrenheit but may be stored at as low as 45 degrees or as high as 70 degrees without undue harm. The important thing to avoid is abrupt changes in temperature.

Wines should also be kept out of bright light, in fact, the less light the better. The same advice applies to movement... the less the better.

USING THE LEFTOVERS

The dinner is over, the guests have gone. Still remaining in the bottle are some remnants of the evening's libations.

There are two alternatives open: drink it up as things are put back in place and dishes are cleared off, or save it for a later use. The former course is probably more fun, the later more practical but only within certain limits.

Wine is, in a sense, a living organism (unlike distilled liquors), and has a limited life span so make no attempt to store an opened bottle on a long term basis. Here are some ideas of how you can use it to good effect.

Appetizer wines. Because of their added ingredients, these wines will keep longer than any others. Actually you can keep appetizer wines for weeks as long as they are kept corked.

Table wines, on the other hand do not keep well. If you have leftover wine in a 750ml ("fifth") bottle, cork it carefully and store it in the refrigerator for use the next day. It should be used within a week. "Jug wine" left over in a half-gallon or full gallon bottle should be poured into a smaller container and corked, refrigerated and used within a week. The important thing is to let as little air as possible come into contact with the surface of the wine.

Ultimately, leftover table wine can be used in cooking after it has become unpalatable for drinking.

Since we started with a quotation, let's finish with one too. Benjamin Franklin gives us this one: "Wine is constant proof that God loves us, and loves to see us happy." Let's enjoy it.

Chapter 5:

PLANNING YOUR PARTY

There are two very important "indispensable ideas" when it comes to parties.

The first is: PEOPLE MAKE THE PARTY.

Whether it is one or two people, or one or two hundred people the principle is the same... a party happens when people get together to enjoy each others' company, to share, to have fun. Food certainly can add to the pleasure of the occasion... as can music, decorations, and all the other things that come to mind when you think of a party, but without people there just is no party.

We often use the phrase "giving a party" and when you think about it, it is an apt turn of phrase. If you think about a party as a gift to your friends, you are on the right track.

Give your guests a gift of a pleasant time.

Give your guests a gift of good food nicely served.

Give your guests a gift of yourself by having everything ready so that you can be with them.

Give your guests the gift of being at ease.

Give them the gift of the memory of a happy occasion.

The second "indispensable idea" is: SIMPLEST IS BEST.

Tempting though it is to try out an elaborate dessert or elegant table setting... don't. When you plan your menu, include things that you are comfortable with, things you have made before, things that do not take a lot of last minute attention.

As the person hosting the party, you want to be at your best... calm, relaxed, and enjoying yourself. You cannot be any of those things if you are worried about the outcome of one of the dishes you are serving, running back and forth from kitchen to guests.

You can relax and enjoy your own party if you are confident that everything is ready before the doorbell rings to announce the first guest. To make that possible plan ahead, and prepare as many things in advance as you possibly can.

Although every party is different, here is an outline of a schedule for a party that will involve perhaps eight to fifteen guests for some special occasion.

PARTY PLAN

At least two weeks before the party:

Decide on the date and time for the party and make out a list of the people you would like to invite.

Will the time of year or weather affect your plans? Is it a holiday celebration or a special family occasion, a birthday, graduation, promotion, anniversary? Is it the Super Bowl or the final game of the World Series? Would you like to try a "theme party" for friends?

Any of these are possibilities... and an infinite number more only limited by your imagination... if you don't have an "occasion", you can always make one up or pick something from a calendar that cries out to be celebrated... how about the anniversary of the first flight at Kitty Hawk (December 17th), or Mick Jagger's birthday (July 26th) or Ground Hog Day (February 2nd), or the Academy Awards presentation (sometime in April)... the possibilities are truly endless.

Decide what you are going to need that you don't have on hand. If you will need to borrow or rent serving pieces, chairs, or other things, now is the time to make the arrangements.

This is especially true around holiday time at the end of the year. June is another time that you may need to make reservations for rentals well in advance because of the number of graduation and wedding celebrations that will be going on.

For a casual party among friends, relax and don't worry about everything absolutely "matching" or having every single piece of serving equipment, mix patterns and colors and let pieces do double duty.

Two weeks before the party:

Invite your guests. Unless this is a casual drop-in evening among close friends, send invitations or call your guests, find out how many will be free to attend your party on the date you have selected.

Decide on your menu. Here are some things to keep in mind:

> Choose dishes you are confident and comfortable about cooking.
>
> Choose things that will please your guests, this entertainment is a "gift" to them after all.
>
> Choose foods that are suitable for the kind of party you plan. Some foods are just not suitable for buffet serving for instance, while others can be eaten either at table or in a more casual seating arrangement.

Decide how the food will be served... a sit-down dinner with the plates filled in the kitchen or served family-style? A buffet? Where will your guests take their filled plates to be eaten? Will you serve outdoors or indoors... or both by having pre-dinner drinks and appetizers outside followed by dinner inside, or perhaps dessert served outside?

PLANNING YOUR PARTY

A week before the party:

Arrange the things you will need. Set a time and place to pick up any of the things you need to borrow. Call the rental shop and verify the delivery date and time for things you plan to rent. Arrange for any special decorations or flowers.

Choose your recipes. Sit down with your recipes and a notebook, adjust the quantities to serve the number of guests you expect, and make out a complete list of everything you will need. Then, go to your cabinets and cross off the things you have already available. What you have left is your party shopping list. (Don't forget to include things like candles and other non-food items that are all too easy to overlook.)

A day or two before the party:

Do your shopping and prepare whatever food you can make up in advance. The more you can do in advance, the more relaxed you can be on the day of the party. Don't try to freeze dishes ahead that you have not handled that way before, however... some dishes simply do not freeze well and are best prepared just before serving.

Make some extra space in your refrigerator. Take out anything that can safely be stored elsewhere for a day or two. Condense partly filled large containers into smaller units. Use self-locking plastic storage bags where ever you can because they can be tucked into smaller spaces that rigid-sided containers. You'll need all the extra refrigerator storage space you can find. It is impossible to have too much!

Early on the day of the party:

Put candles in the refrigerator to cool. They will burn down more slowly and drip less. (Putting the candles in the freezer is not a good idea because they are likely to crack.)

Do some superficial cleaning (no one will be inspecting the tops of books for dust or looking to see how clean your oven is!) Arrange furniture so that your guests will be able to move around easily. Put out fresh hand towels in the bathroom your guests will use. Will you need to have coasters available for glasses? What about ashtrays?

If you are going to have music... decide what tapes or discs you want to use and put them where they can be accessed easily.

Put the flowers or other decorations you plan to use in place.

Set the table or buffet.

Check your menu to make sure you have everything you need to finish the food and drink preparation. It is much better to make a final trip to the store four or five hours before the party than five or ten minutes before...

INDISPENSABLE IDEA

Mark your house or apartment if your guests have not been there before... a big bow on the mailbox or outside light, a windsock or holiday banner flying from the porch.

Just before the party:

Finish up the food preparation.

Set up the bar.

Take some time to relax before the party starts... have a glass of wine or a cup of tea, relax your shoulders and take some deep breaths.

At the time your have set for guests to arrive:

Start the music and light the candles.

A couple of other comments about party planning...

If you have a number of people you would like to entertain and, for whatever reason, you do not want to have them all in one group, consider the possibility of having two smaller parties on consecutive nights. You can give your home one cleaning, you can often even serve the same menu for both occasions. You can also make efficient use of anything that you may need to borrow or rent.

Remember too that no matter what time you tell your guests, some-one will inevitably be late. Plan the timing of the food preparation so that you allow extra time for that. If, however, the time continues to pass and the guests are obviously going to be very late, so late that your meal will be spoiled, go ahead and serve. When the late-comers finally arrive simply serve them with as little fuss as possible.

MENU PLANNING

Let's back track a little and talk a bit more about menu planning for a party.

Keeping the axiom that "people make the party" in mind, really think about your guests as you are planning the menu. Are they the adven-turous type always interested in trying something new, or are they more conventional and truly prefer traditional and familiar dishes. The Indian curry you love would no doubt please the former but cause the latter some hesitation, while the baked ham with its usual accessory dishes would make the latter feel comfortable and at ease.

The ages of your guests can also affect what you choose to serve... there are probably no more conservative diners than children, and these young guests usually are not hesitant to let you know that they would prefer meat loaf to beef Wellington or fried chicken to chicken breast Cordon Bleu. Older guests also require consideration... often their diets are restricted either because of digestive or health reasons. This is the time for candor... simply ask the person in question if you are not sure whether the menu you plan will be something that the person can comfortably enjoy.

PARTY STYLES

Any kind of gathering of friends can be called a "party" but there are many styles that a party can take. To give you some ideas about ways to plan different party styles, let's look at several.

BUFFETS.

A buffet is a super informal way to serve and probably the most adaptable sort of party you can give. There are a few things to keep in mind however.

Everyone finds it more comfortable to sit down and have a table available while eating. For a buffet you can arrange this in several different ways.

If your dining area will seat the six or eight you have invited, you can have the table completely set except for plates and as your guests fill their plates from the buffet arrangement they can simply take a place at the table.

If you have more guests than your dining area can has room for and more space in another room you can, of course, use as many folding card-tables as you need and can comfortably accommodate. These also can be set up with linens and tableware in advance. Folding TV tables can be used... sometimes for two people to share. Pillows around a coffee-table work well if the crowd is young enough to make getting up and down a reasonable thing to ask.

INDISPENSABLE IDEA

If you've invited a big crowd and have limited space, set up food service in different rooms... appetizers in the living room, salads in the dining area, main dish in the kitchen, desserts back in the living room. This keeps people moving and helps them become acquainted too.

If, for whatever reason, your guests will have to stand to eat, plan your buffet menu so that it is comprised of all "finger-food" and guests will not have to cope with forks or spoons. There are lots of dishes that are normally thought of as hors d'oeuvres that, when served in ample quantity and variety, can make a quite satisfactory meal. Be sure to have at least two or three plates available for each guest though because they may wish to make return trips to the buffet during the course of the evening.

Arrange the buffet service in a logical way so that things can be picked up without backtracking. A sauce meant for meat or pasta, for instance, should come after the meat or pasta dish it accompanies. If guests will be picking up napkins and silver themselves, it usually works out best if they pick them up last.

If you can arrange to do so, it is usually best if someone can serve beverages after your guests are seated.

Desserts can be handled in a variety of ways, all of them casual. You can either set up a dessert table in the room where people are eating or clear the original buffet and plan on serving a dessert late in the evening. Don't feel that desserts are obligatory unless you know that your guests are from the school that feels that no meal is complete without a dessert to "fill in the holes" as an old Dutch saying goes.

INDISPENSABLE IDEA

If you save up pint and half pint dairy containers in advance, they can be used to freeze large "cubes" of ice that will fit into most serving pitchers or can be used in punch bowls. In most cases, however, it really makes more sense to buy bags of ice rather than trying to freeze a large number in your freezer... you have better things to do with your time and freezer space, and commercially frozen ice is also usually clear which makes it attractive.

Finally, a word about food safety when serving a buffet...

Don't forget the cardinal rule of food safety: serve hot foods hot and cold foods cold.

When a buffet is to be out and available for more than two hours, prepare the dishes in smaller containers than can be replaced as they are emptied rather than one large dish where the food can reach and stay at a temperature attractive to unfriendly bacteria.

Borrow extra food warming trays if you need them. Incidentally it is possible to use a waffle iron opened fully, set at the lowest temperature setting, and covered with several sheets of heavy-duty foil for an improvised warming tray.

For summertime parties it is especially important to keep cool foods cool... bacteria particularly love dishes containing mayonnaise or other foods with protein-based components and, although you cannot detect it by just looking at the food, harmful bacteria can multiply at an astonishing and alarming rate.

DINNERS.

"Come over for dinner this weekend" is probably the most common invitation all of us give and receive. Dinner parties when a few friends can sit around a table together are justifiably the most popular entertaining that we do. Easy to plan, easy to handle, pleasant for everyone. Formal dinners, "big" dinners, little dinners, intimate dinners for two, barbecues, cold dinners on the patio or balcony... pick the dinner party to suit your needs.

Often you will like to have before-dinner drinks and snacks with your guests when they arrive to give everyone a chance to relax and conversation a chance to get started. Keep your before-dinner food simple... you don't want people to fill up before they have a chance to enjoy the meal you have fixed. Generally something as simple as a bowl of nuts or a mixture of nuts, pretzels and other dry snacks are quite enough. It usually works best to have several small bowls rather than one large one so that people can have easy access to them without reaching across each other or having to pass things constantly.

Once you and your guests are comfortably seated at the table, relax and take your time. Don't rush dishes and courses on and off the table, but just let everyone enjoy the food and each others' company.

You might consider the possibility of serving the salad as a separate course. Tossing a green salad at the table and having a selection of condiments for your guests to choose among is a nice starting point for the meal. Have a basket of crackers, bread sticks, or rolls available to go with the salad.

For the main course you can either fill the plates in the kitchen and serve directly to the table or, if you prefer and the dinner is casual, just serve family style by bringing the serving dishes of food to the table and passing them. Whatever you choose to serve, as you plan your menu keep in mind that you, as the host or hostess of the occasion, do not want to spend a lot of time getting up from the table and going back and forth to the kitchen.

Whether you choose to fill the plates or have serving dishes on the table, go through a mental checklist before you announce that dinner is ready to make sure you have everything you had planned... or have you never forgotten the rolls that you put in the oven to warm?

Desserts can be served either at the table when the main courses of the meal are finished, or can be served away from the table in the living room or even outside on a warm evening. If you serve at the table, it is always more pleasant to have all parts of the earlier courses cleared first. You may want to put the silver that will be used for the dessert at the top of the plate when you set the table rather than at the side with the rest of the silver.

If you are serving an after-dinner drink instead of (or in addition to) dessert, put the glasses and a bottle or bottles on a tray that you can bring close to the table to serve.

Here are some "variations" on the Dinner Party style...

Midnight suppers.

When you are going to a performance of some kind... whether it is a hockey game, a concert, a movie, a new video tape, or a school play...

it is fun to get together for something to eat and a chance to talk about what you have seen. And what a great opportunity for a small but elegant meal.

One simple but always well-received menu is just an assortment of cheeses and cold cuts with some special breads and spreads and a cake (perhaps one that would be more than you would want to use as a dessert for a full dinner) for dessert.

Or a bowl of a special soup (maybe traditional French onion or a rich clam chowder?) with an appropriate bread.

Whatever you serve, remember that people are going from your entertainment home to sleep so keep your dishes on the light (and easy to digest) side.

Dessert-and-Coffee.

Here is a way for a very busy person to entertain gracefully. If you feel that planning and executing a full-sized dinner party is more than you want to take on, dessert-and-coffee is the perfect answer.

The dessert can even be something that you pick up at the bakery on your way home from work. Once again, the point is that "people make the party". Incidentally with many people now drinking decaffeinated coffee you might want to have some on hand along with tea and some light semisweet wine and/or after-dinner liqueurs.

INDISPENSABLE IDEA

To make a quick batch of mulled cider for drop-in guests on a cold winter's evening, just add a quart of cider to your coffee maker and put the spices (whole cinnamon, allspice, and cloves) in the basket where the coffee usually goes. Run the cycle and the cider will be flavored. (Be sure to run a cycle of plain water through after the cider and before your next pot of coffee though.)

Potluck Suppers.

Finally let's think about that friendliest and most generous sharing of ourselves and our food, the "come-for-pot-luck" invitation. Here is a situation where specific planning is neither possible nor desirable, it is the spontaneity of the invitation that makes it so appealing to both the person being invited and the person extending the invitation.

These spur-of-the-moment invitations are much easier if you have on hand some extra supplies that can be used either to extend what you had already planned for dinner or else can be used to create a simple meal. If you have two or three such meals in mind you can stock your pantry accordingly and be confident of being able to put together something everyone will enjoy in a matter of minutes.

Here are some things to think about having on hand:

> canned meats and fish (ham, salmon, tuna, crab)
>
> canned soups (cream of chicken, cream of mushroom, consomme, tomato)
>
> frozen vegetables
>
> a variety of pastas
>
> "bread" mixes (biscuit mix, muffin mix, etc.)
>
> canned olives, pickles, and other condiments
>
> a jar or pimentos and/or chili peppers
>
> canned or frozen spaghetti sauce
>
> canned fruit (keep something a little exotic on hand will make a simple fruit dessert special)
>
> or other easy to fix desserts.

Go through this list and sort out which things you need to make up the ready-to-go menus you like and you will be prepared for any impromptu invitation you would like to extend.

INDISPENSABLE IDEA

If you are going to serve poached eggs to a crowd (perhaps in Eggs Benedict for brunch), you can poach the eggs in advance and simply keep them in cold water until needed then just pop them in simmering water for about thirty seconds to warm them through and you are ready to serve them.

COCKTAIL PARTY.

The cocktail party is a chance to bring a lot of people together easily and with a minimum of fuss on your part. Here, as always, just remember it is the people that make the party.

Follow through the pre-party planning outlined at the beginning of this chapter.

Have plenty of hors d'oeuvres but keep the variety within limits. Have some hot and some cold. Keep them easy to eat... no sauces that will spot clothes, no tiny pieces to slip, no large pieces to cut. In fact the ideal food for a cocktail party is food that is truly "finger food" so browse through your cookbooks and recipe collection with those thoughts in mind as you plan your menu.

As you plan your invitation list keep in mind the amount of space you have for people to circulate without bumping into each other. If you have the room for a large number, you will probably find that up to twenty-five guests seem to work as one party... more than that and the party tends to break up into mini-parties of ten or so people each.

A successful cocktail party caters to both the physical and the social requirements of your guests. You need to be ready to introduce strangers and steer newcomers to an appropriate conversation group. You need to keep an eye on supplies and make sure everyone has something to eat and drink. You need to make sure the ventilation is adequate and the ashtrays are plentiful. You need to help people to be comfortable. Remember this is the end of the day, sometimes the end of a work day or a work week, and people want both the relaxation and the stimulation of a party atmosphere.

Wine or beer tasting party.

This is a variation on the cocktail party... usually more casual, relaxed and usually works best with a smaller group... say up to twelve people.

There are several ways this can be done... either the host or hostess buys a selection of wines or beers, or each guest can bring a sample. If you choose the latter, it works best if you tell the guest what general kind of wine to bring... Johannesburg rieslings, pinot noir or merlots, blush or roses, sherries, and so forth so that you really have a basis for comparing them. With beers you might suggest the country of origin for each guest's contribution and let them select the variety.

With the drinks have a variety of appetizers and select them to go with the drink you will be tasting. Cheeses, breads or crackers, pates, crudites are all possibilities.

INDISPENSABLE IDEA

Drop a twist-tie in the bottom of your waste container before you put the plastic bag in. When you pull the bag out to empty it, the tie will be ready to use.

OCCASIONS FOR PARTIES

Holidays are natural times for entertaining but there are lots of other occasions that are cause for celebration... birthdays, of course, but also graduations, christenings, showers for parents-to-be as well as brides-to-be, new job or a move to a new home, promotions or good school grades, special sporting events, retirements, departures on a special trip, a special visitor... to name just a few.

Theme parties are also fun with menu, music and maybe some decorations around a certain idea... a Medieval or Renaissance or Victorian dinner, an Indian or Japanese or Mexican dinner, a trim-the-tree Christmas party or a board-game party.

A little thought and freewheeling imagination and you can come up with a host of entertaining ideas.

Here is a calendar listing a few of the days to celebrate in each month... you'll probably think of others too.

A MONTH-BY-MONTH IDEA LIST OF REASONS FOR A PARTY

JANUARY

1	New Year's Day... football and parades
5	Twelfth Night/Twelfth Day Eve (Christian holiday)
6	Twelfth Day (Christian holiday of Epiphany when the three kings appeared, called Three Kings Day in some countries)
7	Birthday of Millard Fillmore (13th President) (1800)
14	Birthday of Albert Schweitzer (1875)
15	Birthday of Martin Luther King (1929)
19	Birthday of Robert E. Lee (1807)
	Birthday of Edgar Allen Poe (1809)
25	Bobbie Burns Day (birthday of Scottish poet Robert Burns) (1759)
26	Australia Day (national holiday in Australia)
27	Birthday of Wolfgang Amadeus Mozart (1756)
**	Don't forget Superbowl Sunday!

FEBRUARY

2	Ground Hog Day
4	Birthday of Charles Lindbergh (1902)
7	Independence Day for Grenada
12	Birthday of Abraham Lincoln (1809)
	Birthday of Charles Darwin (1809)
14	Valentine's Day
16	King Tut's tomb opened (1923)
19	Patent on the gramophone (phonograph) granted to Thomas Edison (1878)
22	Birthday of George Washington (1732)
27	Dominican Republic Independence Day
**	President's Day (US) celebrated third Monday in February

MARCH

2	Texas Independence Day
6	Birthday of Michelangelo (1475)
13	First demonstration of a "talking movie" by Lee de Forest in New York City (1923)
14	Birthday of Albert Einstein (1879)
15	Birthday of Andrew Jackson (1767)
16	First launching of a solid fuel rocket by Robert Goddard (1926)
17	Saint Patrick's Day (Christian holiday)
19	Roman festival of Minerva, goddess of wisdom
21	Vernal Equinox (day and night are equally long, sometimes called First Day of Spring)
**	Easter (Christian holiday) is celebrated on the first Sunday on or after the first full moon on or after the 21st day of March (Orthodox Christian Easter is usually later in the spring)
25	Independence Day in Greece
**	Purim (Jewish holiday) is celebrated in March

APRIL

1	April Fool's Day
5	Ching Ming Festival (Hong Kong and Taiwan)
8	Buddha Day (Buddhist holiday celebrates birth of Gautama Buddha)
12	First successful manned space flight by Yuri Gagarin (1961)
14	Pan American Day
19	Independence Day in Venezuela
22	National Sovereignty Day in Turkey
23	St. George's Day (celebrated in England)
28	Roman festival of the flowers (Floralia)
**	Arbor Day is usually celebrated on the last Friday in April

MAY

1	May Day
5	Children's Day in Japan
7	Independence Day in Israel
17	Constitution Day in Norway
21	Lindbergh arrives in Paris after crossing the Atlantic (1927)
24	Birthday of Queen Victoria (1819)

30   Memorial Day in US (celebrated on the last Monday in May)

**   Mother's Day is celebrated the second Sunday of May

**   Armed Forces Day (US) is celebrated on third Saturday of May

JUNE

3   Birthday of Jefferson Davis (1808)

5   First ascent and successful descent in a hot-air balloon by the Montgolfier brothers (1783)

    Birthday of Pancho Villa (1878)

6   World War II D-Day invasion of Europe

8   Birthday of Frank Lloyd Wright (1867)

    Birthday of Robert Schumann (1810)

11   Kamehameha Day in Hawaii

14   Flag Day

17   Bunker Hill Day (Massachusetts)

21   Summer Solstice (longest day of the year, Northern Hemisphere), sometimes called the First Day of Summer

**   Father's Day is celebrated the third Sunday of June

JULY

1   Dominion Day in Canada

4   United States Independence Day

6   Alaska becomes 49th state

    Birthday of John Paul Jones (1747)

10   Telstar 1, world's first TV satellite launched (1962)

14   Bastille Day in France

15   Bon (Buddhist holiday in Japan, China, Tibet, and Korea)

21   Neil Armstrong is the first man on the moon (1969)

AUGUST

1   Colorado Day

13   Birthday of Alfred Hitchcock (1899)

15   Independence Day in India (1947)

    Birthday of Napoleon Bonaparte (1769)

    Birthday of T. E. Lawrence (Lawrence of Arabia) (1888)

19	Birthday of Orville Wright (1871)
28	Onam (Hindu harvest festival holiday)

SEPTEMBER

7	Birthday of Queen Elizabeth I (1533)
8	First Star Trek episode aired (1966)
9	California becomes a state (1850)
16	Independence Day in Mexico
17	Citizenship Day in US
22	Autumn Equinox (day and night are of equal length, sometimes called the First Day of Autumn)
26	Birthday of George Gershwin (1898)
**	Labor Day in US and Canada is the first Monday in September
**	Grandparent's Day is the first Sunday in September
**	Rosh Hashanah and Yom Kippur (Jewish holidays) occur in September
**	Muharram (the Moslem holiday of the new year) is celebrated in September

OCTOBER

2	Birthday of Mahatma Gandhi (1869)
10	Birthday of Giuseppe Verdi (1813)
12	Columbus Day (US) is celebrated the second Monday in October
14	Battle of Hastings (1066)
24	United Nations Day
27	Birthday of Theodore Roosevelt (1858)
31	Halloween
**	Thanksgiving Day in Canada is the second Monday in October

NOVEMBER

1	All Saint's Day (Christian holiday)
2	First radio broadcast in US in Pittsburgh (1920)
4	Day of National Unity in Italy
11	Veterans' Day in US (Remembrance Day in Canada) Roman feast of Vinalia (honoring Bacchus, the god of wine)
17	First ship sails through the Panama Canal (1913)
22	Birthday of Charles de Gaulle (1890)

23   Labor Thanksgiving Day in Japan
* *   Thanksgiving in the US (fourth Thursday of November)

DECEMBER
1   Independence Restoration Day in Portugal
2   Birthday of Peter Goldmark (inventor of the long-
       playing record) (1906)
5   Birthday of Walt Disney (1901)
16   Birthday of Ludwig von Beethoven (1770)
17   Wright Brothers Day (anniversary of flight at Kitty Hawk,
       1903)
21   Winter Solstice (shortest day of the year Northern
       Hemisphere), sometimes called the First Day of
       Winter
24   Christmas Eve (Christian holiday)
25   Christmas Day (Christian holiday)
26   Boxing Day in Canada and Great Britain
* *   Chanukah (Jewish holiday) occurs in December

For other birthdays (including those of people still living) check any almanac.

A PARTY DIARY

A party diary is simply a way of making notes to yourself about the entertaining you do. It can be as simple or as elaborate as you wish (and have time for) but it is an extremely handy reference to have.

If you decide to keep a party diary, take a small notebook and make a note of the date of the party, your guests, what the occasion was if any, and what you served.

A quick glance back through this diary will help you to plan menus that do not duplicate what you have served a certain group of guests before, and will also give you ideas and reminders about what worked well in the past.

If you want to go into more detail, you can make notes about your guests' food preferences, costs of various items, how your portion planning worked out (did you have too much or too little of anything on hand for the party?)... whatever you think you would find useful when party planning in the future.

PROVISIONS FOR SERVING LARGE GROUPS

To help you plan for serving large numbers of people, here are a few lists and tables.

Food to Serve	10	25	100
Meat Dishes			
Beef, roasted[1]	4 lbs	10 lbs	40 lbs
Fish, whole[3]	5 lbs	13 lbs	50 lbs
Fish fillets	3 lbs	7 lbs	30 lbs
Ham	4 lbs	10 lbs	40 lbs
Hamburger	3 lbs	7 lbs	28 lbs
Meat loaf[2]	2 lbs	5 lbs	18 lbs
Pork chops[3]	4 lbs	10 lbs	40 lbs
Turkey/chicken[3]	10 lbs	16 lbs	65 lbs

[1] - boneless cut
[2] - weight after cooking
[3] - with bone in

	10	25	100
Sandwiches[4]			
Bread	20 slices	50 slices	200 slices
Butter	1/4 lb	1/2 lb	1 1/2 lbs
Mayonnaise	1/2 cup	1 cup	4 cups
Mixed filling	2 cups	6 cups	24 cups
Lettuce	1 head	2 heads	5 heads

[4] - allowing 1 sandwich per person

	10	25	100
Salads			
Potato salad	2 quarts	4 1/2 quarts	4 1/2 gallons
Pasta salad	1 1/2 quarts	3 quarts	3 gallons
Fruit salad	1 1/2 quarts	3 quarts	3 gallons
Green salad	2 1/2 quarts	7 quart	7 gallons
Cole slaw	1 1/2 quarts	3 quarts	3 gallons

	10	25	100
Vegetables			
Beets, canned	1 no. 3 can[5]	1 no. 10 can[6]	4 no. 10 cans[6]
Carrots[7]	2 lbs	6 lbs	24 lbs

Food to Serve	10	25	100
Corn, canned	1 no. 3 can[5]	1 no. 10 can[6]	4 no. 10 cans[6]
Corn, frozen	4 10 oz pkgs	3 40 oz pkgs	10 40 oz pkgs
Peas, fresh[8]	7 lbs	18 lbs	70 lbs
Peas, frozen	4 10 oz pkgs	3 40 oz pkgs	10 40 oz pkgs
Potatoes, scalloped	1 1/2 qts	4 1/2 qts	17 qts

  [5] - 46 oz can
  [6] - 106 oz can
  [7] - fresh
  [8] - fresh still in pod

BAR SUPPLY CHECKLIST TO SERVE ABOUT 24 GUESTS

These are, of course, only suggestions. What you actually will need will depend entirely on what drinks you plan to serve.

In general people do not expect a wide variety of exotic drinks... keep our "simplest is best" motto in mind. However it is sometimes fun to offer something special such as Pina Coladas in the summer or Egg Nog at holiday time. If you plan to key your party to one special drink, be sure to have some of the standard liquors and mixes, and wine and beer, on hand for the people who prefer an old favorite though. This is a generous list and you'll probably have some left over, but it is better to be over-supplied than under-supplied.

Bar Fruit:
3 Oranges
3 Limes (6 in summer)
3 Lemons (for twists)
1 bottle Maraschino cherries
1 bottle large stuffed olives
1 bottle cocktail onions

Mixes to serve 24 guests:
Club soda 6 liters
Tonic water 6 liters (10 in summer)
Ginger ale 3 liters

Lemon-lime mix 6 liters
Cola 18 cans
Diet soft drinks 24 cans
Tomato juice 1 quart or large can (3
    qts. if serving brunch)
Orange juice 2 quarts (3 if serving
    brunch)
Pineapple juice 1 quart
Grapefruit juice 1 quart
Large pitcher of water (not iced)

Seasonings:
Worcestershire sauce
Tabasco sauce
Grenadine
Dry vermouth (French)
Sweet vermouth (Italian)
Pina colada mix (probably summer
    only)
Hot rum mix (winter only)
Rose's lime syrup
Simple syrup
Nutmeg
Salt and Pepper

Equipment:
Ice bucket (Use a large punch bowl
    on the bar, store extra ice in a
    wastebasket lined with a plastic
    trash bag near the bar.)
Jigger or shot glass
Bar spoons
Can opener
Strainer
Water pitcher
Stirrers
Corkscrew
Knife for bar fruit
Small cutting board
Blender (if pina coladas or frappes
    are going to be offered)

Supplies:
Ice (figure about 1 pound of ice per
       guest plus an additional 20
       pounds)
Wiping towels
Napkins (at least 60)
Glasses (if possible standardize on
       one size and style for instance
       an all-purpose 8 ounce wine
       glass)
Short cocktail straws (if appropriate)
Toothpicks

INDISPENSABLE IDEA

Your washing machine can make quite an adequate over-sized ice-bucket for chilling bottles. Fill it about a quarter full of cold water, add ice and bottles to be chilled. To drain, when all the bottles have been removed, just put the setting on "spin".

Liquors to serve 24 guests:
Scotch 2 liters (3 in winter)
Bourbon 1 liter
Gin 1 liter (3 in summer)
Canadian Whiskey 1 liter
Vodka 2 liters (3 in summer)
Light Rum 1 liter (2 in summer)
Dry sherry 1 liter
Wine, white 8 liters
Wine, dry red 4 liters
Beer 12 cans or bottles (24 in
summer)

(This may seem like a lot, and it is not necessary to have this entire list. You know what your guests are likely to want to have to drink... just be comfortable that you have enough to meet requests adequately.)

To calculate your liquor requirements another way, there are about 26 ounces of liquor in a fifth (750 ml). If you allow one ounce per drink, you can expect to serve about twenty-four drinks from each bottle. If you serve more generously (a jigger is one and a half ounces), reduce your expectations accordingly.

For parties of varying sizes, here are some approximate calculations:

If you're entertaining	Pre-dinner Cocktails	For a Party
4 Guests	8-12 drinks	12-16 drinks
6 Guests	12-18 drinks	18-24 drinks
8 Guests	16-24 drinks	24-32 drinks
12 Guests	24-36 drinks	36-48 drinks
20 Guests	40-60 drinks	60-80 drinks
40 Guests	80-120 drinks	120-160 drinks

SIZES AND SERVING YIELDS OF WINE FROM VARIOUS SIZED BOTTLES:

Split bottle - - - - 2 glasses
Half bottle - - - - 3 glasses
Fifth - - - - 6 glasses (26 ounces total)
12 bottle case of fifths - - - - 72 drinks/case
Magnum - - - - 12 glasses (52 ounces total)
6 bottle case of magnums - - - - 72 drinks/case
Jeroboam - - - - 24 glasses (104 ounces total)

KNOW YOUR LIQUEURS

An small after-dinner drink is often served instead of a dessert. There is a wide array of these sweet drinks to choose among. (We have already talked about some of the after-dinner wines in the last chapter.) Here is a list of the more familiar liqueurs and their flavors:

Amaretto . . . . Almonds
Anisette . . . . Licorice (anise seed)
B&B . . . . Brandy and Benedictine
Benedictine . . . . Herbs and citrus
Calvados . . . . Apples
Chartreuse . . . . Mace, cinnamon, hyssop,
angelica, and balm
Cointreau . . . . Oranges
Creme de cacao . . . . Chocolate and vanilla
Creme de cassis . . . . Black currents
Creme de menthe . . . . Mint
Curacao . . . . Orange peel
Drambuie . . . . Scotch whiskey, honey, herbs
Fiori d'Alpi . . . . Floral (alpine flowers)]
Forbidden Fruit . . . . Brandy and citrus
Frangelico . . . . Hazelnuts
Goldwasser . . . . Brandy, herbs, and bits of gold
Grand Marnier . . . . Brandy and oranges
Jagermeister . . . . Herbs, bittersweet
Kahlua . . . . Coffee
Kirschwasser . . . . Wild cherries
Kummel . . . . Caraway
Liqueur de Framboise . . . . Raspberries
Liquore Strega . . . . Licorice
Maraschino . . . . Maraschino cherries
Noyaux de Cerises . . . . Cherry stones
Ouzo . . . . Licorice (Greek Anisette)
Peppermint Schnapps . . . . Peppermint
Peter Heering . . . . Cherry
Picon . . . . Brandy, quinine, herbs
Prunelle . . . . Plums
Sabra . . . . Orange and chocolate
Slivovitz . . . . Plums
Tia Maria . . . . Coffee, rum, cinnamon, mace
Triple Sec . . . . Oranges and brandy
Van der Hum . . . . Tangerine

YOUR GUEST LIST

That "people make the party" has been one of the themes of this chapter. Let's look at that a little more closely.

Some wise and successful party givers say that the best parties are like the best stews, full of a variety of ingredients and seasoned with some interesting flavors. Think back to the best parties you have gone to... weren't they often made up of a wide variety of people? Don't feel that school teachers only want to talk to other teachers, or neighbors to other neighbors. Mix things up. Invite people of varying ages, interests, professions, and backgrounds. Let them find each other. Certainly you will have some who sit in the background and mainly listen... but think about it, do you really want everyone to be a dazzling conversationalist?

Ask some people you don't know well but would like to know better.

Ask some people you think someone else at the party would like to know. The worst case is that the chemistry doesn't work and you will certainly be able to survive that. The best case is that everyone will call to say what a terrific time they had.

Entertaining takes effort, but the pleasure that it gives to everyone, guest and party-giver alike, makes it worth any effort involved. The more entertaining you do, the more relaxed and confident you will be about it and the more people will look forward to receiving your invitations.

Chapter 6:

THE COOK'S GUIDE TO WEIGHTY MATTERS

Have you noticed that just about everyone is trying to lose weight? Perhaps that is a bit of an exaggeration but losing weight is certainly something of a national pastime if you can judge by the number of books and articles on the subject that seem to appear constantly.

In this chapter there is no attempt to give calorie, carbohydrate, or cholesterol counts. There are no elaborate and regimented menus guaranteed to remove five pounds a week. There are no magical insights into ways that you can eat anything you want as often as you like and still lose weight.

What the chapter does have are some ideas and thoughts for the person who cooks for weight conscious people. It includes some ideas that have been effective for others and can be worked into your everyday preparation of food in a way that becomes almost second nature.

Although the medical research jury is still out, and new information constantly adds to our knowledge of the causes and effects of excess weight, it seems hard to dispute that ultimately our weight is determined by how much we use of what we eat. What our bodies do not need to use to produce energy for activities, growth and maintenance is converted into nature's very effective energy storage material: fat.

Therefore, generally speaking and on the most basic level, there are two ways to reduce the amount of fat our bodies store: eat fewer calories or use up more.

Calories, by the way, have an instant association with weight loss and perhaps it would be useful to include something about calories, what they really are, and how they are measured.

The original concept of the word calorie was taken to mean "gram calorie". A gram calorie is the amount of heat that is needed to raise the temperature of one gram of water one degree in the Celsius temperature measurement system.

Because a gram calorie is a very small unit, the kilocalorie (1000 gram calories) has become the standard unit of measurement used by researchers and it is this measurement that is almost always meant when you see the term "calorie" used regarding diet and weight loss.

Strictly speaking then, a calorie is a measure of heat, and not directly related to nutrition. It comes into kitchen terminology because our bodies use the food taken in as fuel to produce energy. Although the theories regarding weight gain and loss become steadily more complex, there seems to be agreement that an excessive intake of "fuel", as measured by calories represented in food eaten, will result in the body storing the excess for later use. From a simplistic view, it is this storage procedure that adds undesirable inches in the form of body fat.

So the question for the cook is: how to keep the calories under control.

There is one bit of information that you need to remember: in an equal volume, fat will have twice as many calories as either carbohydrate or protein. For example, a tablespoon of butter has about twice as many calories as a tablespoon of sugar, or a tablespoon of egg white. (Butter is about 100 calories per tablespoon, egg white is 51 calories per tablespoon, and granulated sugar is 45 calories per tablespoon.)

When you are cooking the effect of this is that the more you can reduce the volume of fat in meals, the more calories you are cutting out.

INDISPENSABLE IDEA

Remember that as your dieters decrease calories, the calories they do take in have to be high in nourishment. In addition to making sure that food is rich in vitamins and minerals, this also may be the time to consider vitamin and mineral supplements if they are not already being taken.

Another basic fact to keep in mind is that water has no calories at all. You may say that is obvious and so what? The implication of calorie-less water is that whenever possible you can extend the volume of food by adding water... more volume, fewer calories per volume unit. For example, almost any prepared salad dressing that you purchase can be thinned with water (depending on the dressing, you can add easily add two tablespoons of water to each cup of dressing), just mix the water in well by shaking or stirring well.

With these two ideas, an astonishing number of calories can be cut in any given meal.

One of the mainstays of the dieter's menu plan is chicken... and an excellent food it is too. Chicken is versatile, adapts well to almost any international cuisine, is low in cholesterol and high in protein.

Unfortunately, most of the fresh chickens you are offered at the supermarket were raised not in the open where they could exercise as they wandered around all day, but rather in "chicken factories" where they are force-fed and kept in restricted quarters so that all they do is hang around and get fat. Their accumulated fat is what the dieter needs to avoid.

The good news is that most of the significant fat on a commercially grown chicken is found in two places: directly under and attached to the skin, and around their tails. By removing the skin you take away the first and expose the second.

Skinning a chicken is very easy.

Step one: Use a sharp heavy knife and cut off the wings at the shoulder joint.

Step two: With your sharp knife cut in a straight line through the skin from the neck to the tail in the back and from the top to the bottom of the breast in the front.

Step three: Put down the knife and hook the forefinger of your left hand (if you are right handed) through the little circle of bone near the point where the wings have come off. Hold it firmly in your left hand and with your right hand just tug on the skin and pull it down. It will slip away and finish, inside out, at the bottom of the leg. Do the same on the other side and you have a skinned chicken as easy as one-two-three. Sometimes the skin doesn't come off in one piece, but it is still easy to pull it off as long as you have a firm grip at the top.

With the skin removed you can see the small and large accumulations of yellow fat. Just cut them off.

After removing skin and extra fat you are left with one of the best kinds of meat dieters, or anyone else, can eat.

Needless to say, calories are kept low by simmering, steaming, poaching, or baking. Fried chicken, especially commercially prepared frozen fried chicken pieces are loaded with calories but there are so many other ways to fix chicken that you probably won't even miss that old favorite.

Turkey is another great food for dieters with all of chicken's versatility and high nutrition. Turkey has become so popular in recent years that it is available in many forms besides the gigantic oven-filling bird of past years: small young birds, parts only (such as breasts or legs), boned breasts, ground turkey, and so forth. Medium to large birds are still the most economical to buy, however.

Unless you plan on dramatically presenting the roasted bird at the table for carving, consider simmering the turkey you buy. This works particularly well with smaller birds but also can be done with a large bird if you cut it into pieces. Simmering gives you not only a lot of moist meat and but also a huge pot of stock that is ideal for soups and gravies.

Foods that contain "hidden fats" are a potential problem for the dieter and there are many foods that contain more fat that you might suppose. Consider, for example, this short list of foods that contain a full tablespoon of fat (100 calories) in addition to their carbohydrate and/or protein calories:

> 1 ounce of almonds
> 2 cups of whole milk
> 2 ounces of corn chips
> 2 whole large eggs
> 1 ounce sunflower seeds
> 1 regular frankfurter
> 1 1/2 ounces processed American cheese
> 1 croissant

In general, in food whose consistency is dense, whose outside is crisp, or whose texture is smooth, you are probably looking at extra calories. If you want or need to avoid those extra calories, you can find quite acceptable exchanges for the sort of foods you should avoid. For instance:

Instead of:	Have:
Almonds	Popped corn
Whole milk	Low-fat (1 percent) milk
Corn chips	Baked tortilla strips
Whole eggs	Combine 1 whole egg and 1 egg white
Sunflower seeds	Pretzels
Regular frankfurter	Turkey or chicken frankfurter
American cheese spread	Pureed and seasoned cottage cheese
Croissant	Bran muffin or whole wheat toast

Here are some additional ideas for reducing fat when you cook...

Instead of:	Use:
Frying in oil	A non-stick fry pan and oil spray or poach in a little stock
Oil-based salad dressing	Oil-free dressing, vinegar or lemon juice

Mayonnaise-based dressing	Yogurt, buttermilk, or pureed cottage cheese
Sour cream	Yogurt
Regular hamburger	Lean or extra lean ground beef
Ground beef	Ground turkey or chicken
Oil-packed canned tuna	Water-packed canned tuna
Regular cream cheese	Neufchatel "cream cheese"
Standard white sauce	White sauce made with dry skim milk, flour, and butter substitute (Butter Buds)

INDISPENSABLE IDEA

Encourage dieters to drink six to eight glasses of water a day. Drinking water actually discourages fluid retention because the body doesn't program itself to store a supply of water, but instead sets the kidneys up to process fluids right out of the system. By activating the kidney in this way the liver can devote itself to metabolizing fat. A full glass of water before a meal will also help the dieter to have a slightly full feeling before sitting down to eat.

OTHER IDEAS FOR EASY WAYS TO CUT SOME OF THE FAT FROM YOUR MEAL
(and never have it missed!)

Cook vegetables in chicken or beef broth instead of sauteing.

When scrambling eggs, use two egg whites to each egg yolk.

When making breads, substitute two egg whites for each egg called for.

Keep meat portions around three ounces, and in casseroles and stews cut to even less and replace the difference with more vegetables.

Measure carefully the oil used for stir-frying and use the least amount you can. If you spray the pan with oil-spray before adding the liquid oil, you can used even less oil.

INDISPENSABLE IDEA

Here are six ways to prepare fat free sauces:

1. Chill the liquid overnight and allow the fat to rise to the surface and congeal. It can easily be lifted off.

2. Pour the liquid into an empty wine bottle. The fat will rise to the top where it can be poured off without losing any of the other liquid.

3. To quickly remove a lot of the fat, set the pan slightly off the burner, enough that it is slightly tipped. The fat will accumulate on the low side of the pan and can be spooned out pretty well from there.

4. Spread a paper towel on the top of the liquid, a lot of the fat will attach to the towel which can then be lifted off (carefully because it will drip) with tongs or a spatula.

5. Wrap a couple of ice cubes in a towel and skim them over the top of the liquid. A lot of the fat will cling to the towel (but not all).

6. Put a large cold lettuce leave on the top of the food. Leave it there for about three to five minutes and it will allow you to lift out a surprising amount of fat but, again, not all.

Cut meats into small pieces whenever possible so that visible fat can be removed (stir-fry, stews, stroganoff, casseroles and soups are all places where this can be done).

Use dry powdered milk and water instead of whole milk in all cooked recipes that call for milk as an ingredient.

Use butter substitutes granules or "diet" margarine. The granules are made primarily from milk solids while the calories in "diet" margarines are cut in half by beating water into the solid margarine).

Use low calorie mayonnaise and other prepared dressings, and use the least you can of those too.

Distribute small amounts of salad dressing by really tossing or mixing well. You will be surprised how little you can use and still have a tasty salad.

When you prepare chicken or beef stock always cook it at least one day ahead so that you can drain the liquid into a container and chill. Chilling will cause the fat to rise to the top and congeal making it simple to remove.

Cook with low fat cheese whenever you can do so without changing the taste and texture of the dish too much.

When you serve low calorie margarine on vegetables, put a small amount on each serving, don't put the margarine on the table.

Always buy lean meat cuts. More and more are available as meat packers respond to buyer's demand for leaner meats. Try some of the turkey and chicken processed meat substitutes (franks, pastrami, and so forth).

If you like cream or milk with your coffee or tea, try using dried skim milk instead. It is easy on calories, easy to carry to work, and easy to store.

Fill up on high fiber vegetables (including potatoes, whole grains and salads) to feel satisfied when you leave the table.

CHARACTERISTICS OF FOOD WE GET FROM PLANTS

In general, when you are choosing foods for a weight-loss menu, keep in mind the "original" purpose of the food. Roots, for instance, sustain the plant and promote growth of leafy parts. Roots therefore are storehouses of energy and are going to be higher in calories than the part of the plant that grows above the ground. (Potatoes, onion, carrots, beets, and others).

Similarly seeds (and in this sense we'll include nuts too) need to provide enough fuel/energy for the plant to germinate and be sustained until roots can be established. Seeds also have to be small and light weight compared to the size of the mature plant. Seeds therefore store their fuel/energy in the form of oils (fats) because more energy can be compressed into less space. The bottom line is that seeds and nuts are high in calories. (Peanuts, sunflower seeds, walnuts and other nuts, wheat and other grains)

In case you've ever wondered why salads are a dieter's mainstay... perhaps this information will help explain it. It may also help explain why the extras that we add at the salad bar can undo our good intentions... a spoonful of sunflower seeds or grated cheddar (or both!) is enough to turn a low-cal salad into something not-so-low-cal at all.

All is not lost, however, because there are a surprisingly large number of things that make good snacks and treats... not brownies or potato chips, of course, but something to help "fill in the holes" without filling out the waistline:

Under 100-calorie snacks

1/2 cup pears packed in juice
1 cup light canned fruit cocktail
1/2 cup fresh cherries and 2 table-
    spoons vanilla yoghurt
1 small apple
1 cup unsweetened applesauce
1 small Bartlett or Bosc pear
3/4 inch slice of fresh pineapple and
    2 tablespoons of Pina Colada
    yoghurt
1 cup fresh strawberries and 1 table-
    spoon of powdered sugar
25-30 roasted pistachio nuts
5 fresh apricots or 7 dried apricot
    halves
20 large spears of steamed asparagus
1 small banana (about 8 inches long)
    or half a large banana
7 saltine crackers (2 inch square)
3 graham crackers (2 1/2 inch square)
1/2 toasted bagel (plain)
10 large stalks of celery
25 grapes (try freezing them first)
2 taco shells

> 1 cup low fat milk (skim or 1 percent)
> 4 ounces of champagne, red or white
>   table wine
> 12 ounces of "light" beer
> 1 cup of buttermilk
> 1 cup lo-cal cranberry cocktail
> 1 1/2 cups watermelon cubes

By scanning books containing lists of calories, you can develop your own list of OK foods for yourself and the other dieters you cook for. Keep plenty of those safe snacks on hand to ease those moments of craving that every dieter has.

If you plan a week's menu schedule at a time you can do several things, not the least of which is get an overall picture of calorie intake during the day and through the week. As you make those plans, here are some ideas that may help add some variety while continuing to stay on the lean path.

BREAKFASTS

Low fat cottage cheese and fruit make a quick, high protein breakfast that can be eaten on the run... fruits can be anything you like but crushed pineapple, peaches (fresh or canned in juice), or chopped apple (with some nutmeg on top) are particularly good. You can also substitute low-fat yoghurt for the cottage cheese but be aware that the pre-sweetened flavored yoghurts are not particularly low in calories even though they may be labelled as "low fat".

French toast or pancakes cooked in a no-stick pan that has been sprayed with vegetable oil spray, and served with unsweetened applesauce and dusted with cinnamon is filling and delicious.

If you eat a piece of fresh fruit instead of drinking juice, you will have a greater sense of "eating"... plus the benefit of the extra fiber in the whole fruit.

Take your morning vitamins with low-fat milk instead of juice, you'll get some protein and calcium instead of just carbohydrates.

If you've been accustomed to drinking homogenized (4 percent) milk, don't try to drop down to skim milk in one step. Instead start out with 2 percent for a few weeks, then 1 percent and finally skim. By that time drinking homogenized milk will seem like drinking cream.

A poached egg on a half toasted English muffin with a generous dash of paprika or parmesan cheese is satisfying and tasty.

If you like an omelette for breakfast, omit all but one egg yolk and use steamed leftover vegetables, mushrooms, or spanish sauce instead of cheese as a filling. Mix in some fresh or dried herbs too.

Watch out for no-cholesterol imitation "sausage"... the cholesterol may be missing, but the calories aren't. Always read the label of any food that calls itself low-fat or "light" to make sure the actual calorie count is something you can live with.

Instead of high sugar content jams and jellies, look for spreads that contain no sugar, or use pureed baby fruits, or better still, make your own fruit spread by putting frozen fruit in the blender and pureeing. Apple butter has some sugar but not so much you couldn't enjoy it occasionally.

When you use diet margarine on your toast, let the toast cool before spreading the margarine. Because of the water content of diet margarine, it can make warm toast soggy but works just fine once the toast has cooled.

Scrape a jar of room temperature peanut butter out into a bowl and add as much wheat bran as the peanut butter will hold without becoming stiff then put the mixture back into a large container (larger than the original one as the volume will have increased). This not only cuts down on the calories in each spoonful, but also makes it easier to spread when you take it from the refrigerator and will add some desirable fiber to the diet.

If your dieters long for an occasional taste of bacon or sausage, use just one piece but cut it into small sections, fry it, drain off all fat and then add the cooked pieces to scrambled eggs.

Hot cereal makes an excellent breakfast... filling, low calorie (especially when served with low-fat milk), and high in fiber which dieters need to feel full and also to keep their digestion on track.

LUNCHES

If you like salad bars, help yourself... to lots of greens but go very easy on the dressings and toppings. (A tablespoon of sunflower seeds can contain as many calories as the rest of the salad put together!) Remember too that although potato salad and macaroni salad have "salad" as their last names, they are still basically potatoes or macaroni mixed with plenty of mayonnaise, and it is probably best to pass them by.

Look for half sandwiches on the menu and if you have a choice of soup or salad always opt for the salad and ask for oil and vinegar dressing on the side... skip the oil, put on all the vinegar you like and season with some pepper. (Or taper down on the oil little by little--soon you won't even miss it.)

Many restaurants offer a "low-cal" luncheon plate but often these are no bargain for the dieter because they consist of a hamburger patty, cottage cheese and maybe a slice of tomato. You are really better off with a dinner salad and a roll, or a bowl or soup and some crackers.

If you eat a burger at a fast food restaurant, you can significantly decrease the calories if you cut the meat patty in half and eat the half meat serving on the whole bun. Most of the calories are in the fat that is contained in the hamburger meat.

For brown-baggers, a 3-4 ounce can of tuna, chicken, salmon, or shrimps makes an excellent lunch. If a refrigerator is available for storage till lunch time, make your own tartar sauce by mixing a little pickle relish with some yoghurt or low-cal mayonnaise and lemon juice. One or two bread sticks and some fresh vegetables or fruit will round out the meal.

Another possibility is to carry a spinach salad in an airtight plastic bag and a small container of diet dressing. Such a salad is both filling and loaded with iron. (Most women can use can use the extra iron.) A hard-cooked egg grated into the salad adds extra protein.

Look for low calorie cheeses, luncheon meats (especially turkey based processed meats), and naturally low calorie foods such as chicken and turkey breasts. Any of these can be taken in slices or cut into chunks and threaded on a wooden skewer for easy eating. Keep these foods as cool as possible, ideally in a refrigerator.

Fresh fruits are wonderful for a light lunch... add a piece of cheese or a half cup of cottage cheese (carried in a small thermos container if you don't have a refrigerator for storage) and you will have all you want.

INDISPENSABLE IDEAS

Encourage your dieter to always leave something on the plate... discourage membership in the "clean-your-plate club". Dieters should train themselves to stop when they have had enough, not when their plate is empty.

DINNER

Review the ways for keeping fat out of your food that were mentioned above... they all apply to dinner preparation.

Use your steamer often... you'll find it is a great way to retain the flavor as well as the valuable nutrients in vegetables, and can be used for fish and poultry too. (A fringe benefit is that the water used for steaming becomes a lightly flavored broth, simmer it to reduce the volume and intensify the flavor and use it as you would any stock.)

If you like baked potatoes, eat only a half... share the other half with someone else or save it for another day. A reasonable substitute for sour cream can be made by making a smooth puree of a half cup of low-fat cottage cheese and a little lemon juice. Top with some fresh or dried chives or dill and you have saved at least half the calories of the same amount of sour cream. Another baked potato trick you might try is to grate some Parmesan, Romano, or other hard cheese on top of the potato and put it under the broiler for a minute or two. (A tablespoon of hard cheese is about 25 calories.)

When you do a pot roast, cook it the day before you plan to serve it. Separate the broth from the roast and store them separately in the refrigerator. When chilled you can skim all fat from the broth and make a tasty but low-fat gravy (to thicken it use cornstarch instead of flour and, because you use less, you will save a few calories there too).

INDISPENSABLE IDEA

If a sauce, broth, or gravy looks a little anemic, don't be afraid to add some color. Yellow food coloring will add a rich, buttery look to white sauces or anything made with chicken broth. Use gravy coloring or instant coffee granules to color anything a little browner. By fooling the eye, you can trick your brain into believing that you are eating a nice rich dish.

Use mushrooms generously... they are very low in calories unless sauteed in a lot of oil or butter. Instead of that, remove the stems from fresh mushrooms and put them cup side up in a pan with a little olive oil to keep them from sticking. Pour a few drops of lemon juice into each cap and gently saute until golden brown on top. Use the stems in other dishes.

Use all vegetables generously, especially in casseroles, soups, and stews. Often it is the volume that we eat that makes us feel satisfied and that volume can just as well be low calorie vegetables as high calorie meats, potatoes, or pasta. Great vegetables to use for these volume supplementers include celery, mushrooms, green peppers, onions, carrots, cabbage, zucchini, among others. Even spaghetti sauce can be lightened up with a generous amount of celery, green peppers, and onions (and don't forget the garlic!)

Fish is an excellent substitute for red meats. Fish is much leaner, and the fat that it does have turns out to be good for you according to current research. Expand your horizons from sauteed fish into the areas of baked fish, poached fish (hot or cold), or fish kebabs (a combination of a firm fish such as halibut with prawns and scallops makes an elegant barbecue or broiler meal). Fish cook extremely well in the microwave too and can be cooked without any oil that way.

You can cut the calories in meat loaf several ways: use lean ground beef, extend the volume with ground vegetables, cooked rice or bulgur wheat, whole wheat bread crumbs, or oatmeal. Invest in a meat loaf pan in two parts that allows all fat to drain out into the lower part of the pan. Top the meat loaf with seasoned canned tomato sauce.

Another way to extend ground meat is to substitute a cup of cooked lentils for 1/2 pound of ground meat. The lentils are loaded with protein but totally lacking in fat. (This also is a money saver.)

Have fruit for dessert, fresh or canned in its own juice. If you home preserve fruit by freezing or canning, remember that fruit can be preserved without sugar. Add a little artificial sweetener when served if you want to enhance the natural sweetness of the fruit.

When serving guests, a plate of easy-to-eat fruit (such as grapes, apple sections, or pear sections) accompanied by some Brie or other cheese, and perhaps some semisweet cookies makes an always welcome finale to a meal. Your dieter can enjoy just the fruit without making the calorie cutting obvious.

Pies are a problem because there is no way to make a traditional pie crust without fat. However, graham cracker crusts are suitable for many pies. Butter cakes (which means most cake mixes) are also out-of-bounds but angel food cakes and sponge cakes (which do not contain butter or shortening) are not too high, as desserts go, and can be served with fresh fruit in season.

There are a number of fruit ices and sorbets available that also give a sweet finish to a meal without incurring too high a toll of calories.

INDISPENSABLE IDEA

Psychologists tell us that we eat less if the food is served on plates colored grey, green, brown, or light blue. Bright colors like red, yellow and orange tend to stimulate the appetite.

SNACKS, PARTIES, AND OTHER EATING TIMES

Fresh fruits have got to be mentioned again here even at the risk of sounding too repetitious. Check the list of low calorie snacks at the beginning of this chapter for some ideas.

Dried fruit is another good snack food, not as low in calories by volume as fresh fruit because the water has been removed and what is left is the carbohydrate content of sugar and fiber, but dried fruit is tasty and filling, and loaded with good nutrition.

Popcorn is a great snack when popped without oil (or just a tiny amount of oil). There are about 25 calories in a cup of popped corn and it has the added benefit of being high in fiber. Popcorn also lends itself well to other seasonings such as the various mixtures found in the spice and herb section of the store (Italian, Mexican, salad mix and so forth), also is good with a dusting of Parmesan or Romano cheese. Watch out for movie-theater popcorn though because it is loaded with salt and has been popped in oil.

For cocktail party snacks have available things like crudites (raw vegetable pieces), small dry crackers, small pieces of cheese, melon balls, fresh pineapple chunks and other low calorie options.

As dieters choose how to "spend" their daily allotment of calories at these social gatherings, they should be aware of the approximate calorie count in various alcoholic drinks:

Beer, 12 ounce can or bottle......150 calories
Table wine, 6 ounce glass.........150 calories

Fortified wine, 3 ounce glass......120 calories
In each jigger (1 1/2 ounce service) of:
80 proof distilled liquor.........100 calories
90 proof distilled liquor.........110 calories
100 proof distilled liquor.........125 calories

Remember that regular mixes, juices, and other ingredients that go into the drink all increase the calorie count too.

When you are entertaining you will probably want to offer alternatives to alcohol too... vegetable or fruit juice, diet soda, or club soda. You will find that a number of people, and not just dieters, may prefer to skip the alcoholic drinks for health or other reasons.

A final thought about the place of fat in the diet of those you cook for. The American Heart Association has some quite indisputable evidence that most of us eat far too much fat, and that fat consumption is directly tied to an appalling variety of health problems. So in addition to the aesthetic reasons for weight loss, it appears that you will be contributing to the good health and long life of those for whom you cook if you make every effort to keep their fat intake under close control.

THE EXERCISE SIDE OF THE EQUATION

Although this is a book about food and its preparation, a chapter on "weighty matters" really should say something about the other side of the weight-loss equation, using up calories by exercise.

You can calculate in a general way the number of calories needed for weight maintenance with this formula: from a height-weight chart, pick a mid-range weight for your height, multiply this figure by 18 for men and by 16 for women. The result will be the approximate number of calories used by an "average" adult with "average" activities.

(For example, if you are a woman about 5 feet 5 inches tall, a mid-range weight for you would be 125 pounds. If you multiply 125 by 16 you will come up with 2000, and that would be an acceptable calorie level for you to maintain your current weight with no change in activity level.)

The following list will give you some idea of how various activities compare in approximate number of calories used per hour:

More than 350 calories per hour:
Running (at about 10 mph),
Bicycling (at about 13 mph),
handball, squash, skiing, tennis,
wood chopping, volleyball, roller
skating
From 250 to 350 calories per hour:
Swimming, walking (at about 4
mph), bowling, golf, vigorous
gardening
From 175 to 250 calories per hour:
Bicycling (5.5mph), walking (2.4
mph), carpentry, light gardening
From 100 to 175 calories per hour:
Standing, sitting reading, watch-
ing television or at a desk

What this means is that if you walk for twenty minutes a day instead of watching television for those twenty minutes, you can drop about five pounds during a year even if you make no other change.

INDISPENSABLE IDEA

Plateaus in weight loss are normal for a dieter, especially one who has many pounds to lose. It happens while your body adjusts to its new weight. To get things started down again increase your exercise slightly, decrease your calories by another 100 a day (but shouldn't go below a total of 1000 calories a day), and drink more water.

The number of calories the body requires daily to maintain present weight level is called the "daily calorie requirement". This number, however, is affected by a variety of factors... whether you are a man or a woman, how tall and how old you are, what you do for a living, and what you do for fun.

Generally speaking, men require a greater number of calories to stay at present weight levels because they tend to have a greater proportion of muscle to fat than most women and more energy is used when the muscle proportion is higher.

The larger you are both in height and in skeletal size, the more calories you need to maintain weight.

As we age we need fewer calories for a variety of reasons: we have achieved our full size and are no longer growing, most of us tend to be not quite as active as we were as teenagers, and in general our physical functions tend to slow down little by little. In proportion to height and activity pattern, the most calories are needed by all of us during infancy and adolescence, and for women during pregnancy and lactation.

What we do for a living controls how we spend most of our time... the classic example of the lumberjack versus the desk-worker makes the point. Unfortunately for weight control, many more of us are information workers and desk-bound all of our working hours while manual work becomes less common. We are also both blessed and plagued by labor saving equipment at work and at home. For instance, changing from a manual typewriter where keys are physically pushed down to the ease of using an electric or electronic typewriter or computerized word processor, can make a surprising difference in the amount of energy expended by a typist during a working day.

And then there are our fun-times... watching a tennis match just does not use as many calories as playing tennis however much as we wish it might. Television is a pervasive part of many of our lives but even so we don't need to become glued to the couch for hours. Even if you or your dieter are not up-at-dawn-to-jog, sports oriented people, there are ways of exercising that you might find enjoyable, even habit forming.

Walking, for instance, is an excellent exercise that can be done easily, without special clothes, at any time, and almost anywhere. Walking can often can be worked into a normal day's schedule. If you park your car or get off at a bus or subway stop a few blocks from where you work or shop, you can easily add a mile or so a day to your activity level. Or use a walk as a chance to spend time with your family... its a great time to talk over the day's activities.

To summarize all of this information, here are ten "indispensable ideas" to help you and those you cook for find success in your weight-loss goals:

1.   Eliminate all the fat you can from everything you eat and use water to cut calories when ever possible.

2.   Make sure there is plenty of water and plenty of fresh vegetables and fruits included in your daily menus.

3.   Don't make or buy foods that should be avoided... why put unnecessary temptation in the path of the dieter? Have lots of OK snacks on hand instead of chips, candy, and cheese.

4.   Eat slowly and savor what is eaten... as cook, you can help by using plenty of seasonings and acceptable additions to keep food varied in flavors and textures. Chewy and crunchy food helps to make the dieter feel satisfied.

5.   Use reduced calorie products when you can... more are available all the time and with some experimentation you will find which ones people like and how they can best be used in your meal plans.

6.   Encourage your dieters not to skip meals because there is some good evidence that eating small meals on a regular basis keeps a dieter's metabolism from moving into a "conservation" mode.

7.   Encourage your dieters to weigh only once a week, same day, same time, same amount of clothing. There can be a surprising amount of daily fluctuation due to changes in fluid retention and other reasons, but week by week the scale should keep a steady downward trend.

8.   Help your dieters choose a reasonable and realistic weight-loss goal, and suggest they discuss goals with their doctor or a nutrition counselor to decide if, given their bone structure, those goals are attainable. (We live in a society constantly bombarded with the image of exceedingly slender people... not all of us were designed to be that way.)

9.   Steer your dieters away from fad diets. Alas, there are no miracle foods or food combinations, no miracle pills, no miracle times, no miracles... period. Weight-loss takes commitment, determination, and self-discipline... none of which come easily to any of us.

10.   Exercise will help to convert stored fat to muscle. Current research also indicates that exercise will keep the dieter's metabolism working at high-speed which will help burn up calories all the time. For these reasons, try to find some kind of exercise for yourself and your dieters that is enjoyable and will be followed consistently. Walking is one of the best, easiest, and most convenient exercises for anyone.

Whether you are the one trying to lose weight or you are trying to help someone else to achieve a weight-loss goal, try to be patient. A modest pound or two a week may not seem like much, especially when there are many pounds to be lost, but pounds taken off quickly have an unhappy tendency to return just as quickly. Be patient, lose at a steady rate, retrain your eating and exercise habits to a new, lifelong style of better nutrition and self-care. If you do, you will be setting forth on a path that will lead to a better self-image, a sense of accomplishment, and very possibly a healthier and longer life.

Chapter 7:

MEAL ACCESSORIES

In this chapter we are going to talk about those foods that are "accessories" to a meal. These are the foods that we use in the same way we use accessories when we dress... to enhance, improve, and modify. These foods are not exotic, quite to the contrary, they are those ordinary things we take for granted: bread, coffee, tea, condiments, and so forth. But a good cook does not just take them for granted because they can add sparkle to a meal and luster to a cook's reputation.

BREAD, EVERYONE'S FAVORITE "FOOD ACCESSORY"

In earlier times, bread was an essential part of the daily food intake. Today it has become one of our accessory foods. Like any accessory it can enhance, improve, and modify. Essential? Probably not. Important? Definitely yes.

Bread is one of a small number of foods that is almost complete in itself... protein from the grain, yeast, and sometimes eggs, carbohydrates from the grain, and usually some fat too.

Breads are usually described as being either "quick breads" or "yeast breads". These terms refer to the methods used to make the bread expand or rise. This expansion of the original dough or batter makes the bread easier to chew and therefore easier to digest and the ingredient used to produce this effect is called a leavening agent.

The most common form of leavening used in bread making is commercial baker's yeast (technically known as *Saccharomyces cerevisiae)*, a microscopically small one-celled fungi. This yeast is available either dry in pre-measured packets or in bulk, or in semi-moist cubes to be found in the refrigerated section of your supermarket.

Sourdough breads are made with a starter of slightly tamed "wild" yeast that is stored in an almost liquid, semi-active state in your refrigerator. The yeast is kept alive by being fed a carbohydrate (flour-water) mixture at intervals.

The use of yeast in either form gives bread a unique texture. This texture is produced by the carbon dioxide that is a by-product of the yeast as it metabolizes the carbohydrates of the flour. This gas is caught in tiny cells formed by a protein factor in flour called that is called gluten. As these cells expand and multiply the dough rises. This process takes the proper temperature (80 to 95 degrees Fahrenheit is ideal) and time (an average batch of bread dough will rise adequately in about an hour).

You may be tempted to use more yeast than is called for in your recipe to speed up the process, but too much yeast not only coarsens the texture of the bread but also causes the loaf to become stale rather quickly.

The correct amount of commercial baker's yeast is about one level teaspoon of dry yeast to three cups of flour. For each additional three cups of flour, however, add only about 1/2 teaspoon additional yeast. Incidentally, most yeast doughs can be covered with plastic wrap and stored in the refrigerator for a day or two after the initial rising but before baking. After refrigerator storage be sure to bring the dough up to room temperature before putting in the oven.

Incidentally, in case you wonder about the yeast... all of the yeast cells are killed by the heat of the oven when the bread is baked.

Quick breads use baking powder instead of yeast to achieve lightness and digestibility. Baking powder available in stores today is what is called "double acting" baking powder.

Baking powder is a combination of baking soda (sodium bicarbonate) and cream of tartar (potassium bitartrate). If you recall some elementary chemistry, you will remember that when liquid is combined with a dry mixture of acid and alkali, carbon dioxide foams off. This is the first action of double acting baking powder. The second action occurs when heat is applied to the batter. The heat causes the gas to expand and, because the gas is trapped in the batter, the expansion adds "air" and lightness to the batter. Leavening by using baking powder is achieved without the long waiting period of a yeast bread so bread products of this type are called "quick breads".

There are also breads that are not put through any sort of leavening process before baking. These breads are described as being unleavened or unraised. The traditional Jewish bread, matzo, is in this category as are the Mexican tortilla and the Indian chapati.

A wide variety of methods are used to cook the raw bread... bread can be grilled, fried, steamed, boiled, boiled and then baked, baked in a pan or on a flat sheet, and in an almost infinite variety of shapes and sizes.

"NOW SHOWING AT A BAKERY NEAR YOU... "

What follows is certainly not a definitive list of bread types, but rather a brief description of the breads you are most likely to find mentioned in recipe books and for sale in large markets and stores that carry ethnic and "gourmet" foods. You can enliven any meal very easily by serving an unusual bread. Sandwiches, too, benefit from some variation. That old-time humorist-philosopher, Will Rogers once said "I never met a man I didn't like"... you'll find yourself paraphrasing him and saying "I never ate a bread I didn't like".

Bagels. Bagels are made of a raised dough and look like an overstuffed, rather heavy, doughnut. They are cooked in an unusual way in that after being raised and shaped, they are parboiled before baking. This gives them a very firm, chewy texture.

Biscuit. Biscuits are a quick bread, perhaps the quickest. Easy to make, easy to vary with additional ingredients, and liked by everyone. Biscuit batter is quite thick and can be either dropped by generous tablespoonfuls onto the baking sheet, or the dough can be flattened slightly by patting down to about an inch in thickness and then cut into circles before placing on the pan to bake. The former are called dropped biscuits and the latter cut biscuits for obvious reasons.

Boston Brown Bread. A quick bread that is cooked by being steamed in a mold. Its consistency is heavy and something like an old-fashioned steamed pudding. Made with rye and whole wheat flours and usually some raisins added. It is a very substantial bread and delicious bread that is often served with baked beans.

Bread sticks. Bread sticks are usually based on a yeast dough but there are some that are made from a quick batter. In shape they are stick-like, and crunchy in texture. You can make "pseudo" bread sticks by cutting frankfurter buns lengthwise into quarters or by cutting day-old French bread into long slender pieces and toasting the pieces. Bread sticks are generally eaten as a snack, or with appetizers or soup rather than with the entree.

Chapati. A bread from India that is traditionally baked on a grill over an open fire. The dough is formed into a ball and then patted into a thin, round shape. The heat of the flame causes it to puff up in places and those bubbles cook first so the bread has a somewhat spotted look.

Cornbread. Cornbread is a quick bread based on cornmeal instead of wheat flour (although most recipes you see will include some wheat flour because without the gluten of the wheat to hold things together the cornbread would disintegrate into a mound of crumbs all too easily). Cornbread is coarse in texture, moist or dry depending on the cook's preference, but very flavorful. There are a number of additional ingredients (such as corn niblets, chopped green or chili peppers, and cheese bits) that you can add for variety too.

Crackers. Crackers could be the subject of book themselves because virtually every ethnic cuisine has some to offer. Broadly defined, crackers are breads that can be leavened or not but which are baked in small flat portions. Crackers can be highly seasoned or quite bland and are used for snacks, to accompany soups or salads, or as a base for appetizers. Virtually every grain flour is the basis for some cracker. Incidentally, one of the peculiarities of American and British English is that the British call crackers and cookies "biscuits" (savory biscuits and sweet biscuits respectively).

Crepes. Crepes are a flour-based food that fall somewhere between bread and pasta. The batter is made with more eggs than pancakes, consequently the finished product can be thinner and more pliable than a pancake and is therefore suitable for rolling around a filling or folding up. Crepe batter, unlike baking powder bread batters, should be mixed thoroughly and then allowed to rest for at least an hour before cooking. Crepes can be made well in advance of use and either refrigerated or frozen until needed.

Crumpets. Tea-and-crumpets is a phrase that seems to conjure up British lifestyle for many of us. Crumpets are a griddle-cooked bread. The cakes are cooked on one side only (something that distinguishes it from an English muffin which is cooked on both sides). The side that is not cooked presents a surface full of holes ideally designed for absorbing butter, warmed honey, strawberry preserves, and other good things.

Doughnuts. Tradition has it that doughnuts were invented in the early days of New England where yeast bread dough was sometimes cooked by frying in oil. As you might imagine, these fried lumps of dough were a trifle heavy to say the least, and often times burned on the outside and still raw dough in the center. Some very inventive New Englander perceived that by taking a portion out of the center, more surface would be exposed to the hot fat thereby causing more surface to brown. The ring shaped doughnut caught on quickly and spread in popularity to become a permanent part of American cuisine. Coffee-and-doughnuts is probably the American equivalent of British tea-and-crumpets.

Dumplings. Dumplings are biscuits that are boiled instead of baked. The liquid in which they are boiled is the stock of a stew or soup and the dumplings absorb some flavor from it. Dumpling batter may be flavored with herbs as appropriate for the meal with which they will be served. With dumplings it is essential to follow directions carefully in terms of keeping the pan uncovered at first and then tightly covered to finish cooking so that the batter stays together in large units rather than simply becoming a thickening agent for the stew.

English muffin. Like the crumpet, the English muffin is cooked on a grill instead of being baked in an oven. The English muffin is made from a yeast dough cut into rounds. The rounds are cooked on a medium hot griddle until browned on both sides. English muffins should never be cut with a knife, but rather should be torn apart to expose the rough, absorbent inner surface ideal for holding little pockets of melted butter.

Flatbread. This is a term used primarily with a type of Scandinavian bread product that is too thick to be called a cracker, but also not what is normally thought of as a "bread" because it is very crisp. Whatever its similarities or differences, it is a welcome change of pace and very good with soups, salads, or spreads.

French bread. Breads described as being French or Italian are similar in that they traditionally are baked without oil or eggs. Without the oil these breads do not keep well but are wonderful when eaten fresh. Authentic French bread acquires much of its crustiness from the brick ovens in which it is baked, these ovens are difficult to duplicate exactly at home but that shouldn't deter you from baking this wonderful bread. Both French and Italian breads can be baked in a vast variety of shapes but the most common are the long narrow loaf (baguette) for French bread and a round loaf for Italian bread.

Fritters. Strictly speaking fritters probably are not a bread, but since they are made with a baking powder leavened batter they more or less fall into the quick bread category. What distinguishes fritters from their cousins, pancakes and waffles, is that the batter is used primarily to bind other foods together. The other foods can be vegetables (as in corn fritters), meat or fish (as in clam fritters), or fruit (as in apple fritters). Fritters are cooked either in deep fat or by sauteing.

Graham cracker. Graham crackers were invented and popularized in the early nineteenth century by Dr. Sylvester Graham (1794-1851), a Connecticut parson and early health food advocate as a "health cracker". Made of whole wheat, bran, and sweetened with molasses, the crackers quickly became a favorite. Graham crackers for many of us evoke memories of early school years always in combination with milk... one of those wonderful foods that carry in their flavor a remembrance of things past.

Lovash. An Armenian flatbread, not too different from Indian chapati in taste, texture and cooking method. A bread that is torn rather than cut. Particularly good with spreads and soups.

Matzo. A thin crisp bread that is not only unleavened but also made without salt. The batter is made of flour and water only.

Muffins. Muffins are in the quick bread category and are in fact a variation on a biscuit. The batter is enriched with egg and oil (and sometimes additional flavoring ingredients) and then baked in special pans that cause the finished product to be shaped like a miniature cake with a rounded top. In making muffins, although it is always a temptation to overfill the pan, the temptation should be resisted if the finished product is to be an attractive shape. Be sure your oven is completely preheated before putting the muffins in because they rely on the heat for a significant part of their leavening. If the muffins stick to the bottom of the pan after baking, try resting the warm pan on a wet towel for a minute before trying again. (The cool towel causes the hot muffin to produce a little steam where it touches the pan. That steam will loosen it enough to make removing it easier.)

Pancakes. Also called griddle cakes, hot cakes, flapjacks and a variety of other names, pancakes are made with a thin biscuit batter, usually enriched with an egg. The batter is poured onto a hot griddle, cooked until the edges start to dry out a bit, then turned and cooked on the other side. Pancakes should be turned only once. The temperature of the griddle is extremely important and the traditional way to judge the correct temperature is when a few drops of water will "dance" when splashed on the metal surface. Wheat flour is most frequently used in making pancakes, but they can also be based on corn, rye or buckwheat. American pancakes are thicker than crepes or Scandinavian pancakes.

Pita. Pita is a bread from the Middle East sometimes called pocket bread because, when the dough is placed in the very hot oven which is required to cook pita, the sudden expansion of the dough caused by the heat makes a "pocket" form as the circle of dough swells into something like a ball. When the bread is cooled, the ball subsides but, just like a collapsed balloon, the cavity is still there. We usually add a filling to pita and eat it as a sandwich but in the Middle Eastern countries that developed it, pita is torn and more often used as a scoop or just eaten as it is.

Popover. Another instance of heat being the leavening agent, popover batter is a combination of flour, eggs, and water. The unique shape and texture of a popover is accomplished by pouring the batter into a preheated popover pan (or custard cup). The result is hollow, light, and delicious but must be eaten immediately or it will become tough.

Popadams. Another bread from India, popadams are made with a batter which contains flour from potatoes and lentils and which can be mild or spicy. Popadams are thinner than chapatis but are the same round shape. When purchased already made, popadams are reheated in hot oil to bring out the flavor and puff up the surface.

Pretzels. Pretzels are recognized by their twisted shape and come in a variety of sizes. Like bagels, pretzels are first precooked in simmering water before a final baking. Coarse salt is usually sprinkled on the surface, but there are also varieties of sweet pretzels.

Scones. A rich biscuit from the British Isles where it is made of a thick batter frequently with some currants or raisins added. The batter is shaped into a mound and the mound is cut into quarters before baking. Scones are often times split and toasted before serving with soft butter and fruit preserves.

Sourdough breads. Although most commonly found in a French-style loaf, sourdough batter can be used to make virtually any bread product from waffles to biscuits, even cakes. Its distinctive tangy flavor and sharp-sweet aroma are caused by the natural "wild" yeast that is its leavening agent.

Tortilla. Tortillas are the staple bread of Mexico and much of Central America. Corn tortillas are made of a special corn meal called masa harina, while flour tortillas are made of a wheat flour and water mixture. Like the breads of India, tortillas are unleavened. The dough is patted or pressed into a very thin round shape and then cooked over an open fire or on a griddle. The masa harina is made of specially processed corn and is essential to making authentic corn tortillas. Corn tortillas are usually about seven inches in diameter while flour tortillas are quite a bit bigger, usually twelve to fourteen inches in diameter.

Waffles. There are many apocryphal stories about the origin of the waffle, but whatever its genesis, waffles are a popular bread product usually, but not always, served at breakfast. The batter is similar to that of pancakes but has more oil added to make the product crisper. As in cooking pancakes, it is essential that the waffle iron is heated before pouring the batter into it. Like pancakes, waffle batter can be based on corn or other grains. Dessert waffles made with batter flavored with vanilla or chocolate make an interesting base for a scoop of ice cream. (Chocolate waffles and peppermint ice cream are a choice combination.)

Zwieback. Zwieback is a German bread that is, as the name indicates, twice baked: zwie (twice) - backen (to bake). The bread is baked, usually in rather flat loaves, cooled then cut into fairly thick slices. The slices are put on a tray and baked in a slow oven until they are dried out and crisp.

The Added Touch...

The added touch is what makes your breads different from anyone else's, and certainly different from off-the-shelf products. It is that extra something that you do to your breads before serving that tells everyone you are an imaginative cook.

Dropped Biscuits

Simple biscuit batter baked as it drops from your spoon can achieve a "gourmet food" status with the addition of one or two ingredients.

CHEESE BISCUITS: coarsely grate 1/2 cup of any hard cheese and add to the batter.

HERB BISCUITS: add about 1/4 cup of finely chopped chives, parsley, or other fresh leafy herb or combination or herbs to the batter.

SPICY BISCUITS: add about 1/4 tsp. dry mustard and a teaspoon of some seed (celery, caraway, sesame, poppy, etc.).

ORANGE: grate the zest from an orange and add to the batter (a little sugar in the batter will enhance the fruit flavor).

MEAT-FLAVORED: finely chop cooked ham or bacon and add to the batter. Sausage can also be used but should be cooked and well drained.

Cut Biscuits

Rolled and cut biscuits can be either those you make yourself or those that you buy from the refrigerated section of the grocery store.

INDISPENSABLE IDEA

There is no law that requires cut biscuits to be round...
pat the dough into a rectangle and cut into squares or
diamonds for a change.

CHEESE: Press a cube of sharp cheese into the center of each biscuit before baking.

CINNAMON: Dip each biscuit into melted butter then sprinkle with cinnamon and sugar before baking.

QUICK SWEET ROLLS: Bake the cut biscuits in muffin tins but before putting the biscuit in drop one of the following into the bottom of each round section: a mixture of nuts, honey, and cinnamon; a mixture of crushed pineapple, brown sugar, and a little butter; or a spoonful of jam or marmalade. Be sure to oil the muffin pan sections well so that tasty treats don't stick.

PINWHEELS: Pat the dough into a rectangle about 1/4 inch thick and gently spread it with jam, marmalade, devilled ham, or a soft cheese (olive, pineapple, pimento, etc.). Roll up lengthwise and cut into inch to inch and a half slices. Put each slice in a well-greased muffin tin section and bake.

Leftover Biscuits

If there are leftovers, they can be rewarmed and made palatable again by wrapping tightly in foil or placing in a slightly dampened paper bag and warming in a 350 degree oven for about 10 minutes or by putting in a steamer until they feel warm to the touch. Biscuits can also be split and toasted under the broiler (try spreading the split biscuits with butter and topping with cinnamon-sugar, grated cheese, or a sprinkling of dried herbs. If the biscuits are too stale to save, put them in the blender or food processor and make crumbs.

Muffins

Traditional muffins may be dressed-up with many of the same topp-ings and "bottoms" that are used with biscuits plus these other possibilities:

>...a bit of jam or jelly in the center
>...a cube of hard or cream cheese pressed into the batter
>...a little cooked fruit added to the batter (be careful not to add too much fruit) crushed pineapple, chopped apples, chopped dried fruits of any sort are good choices.
>...various herbs and spices and nuts can also be added.

Be sure not to over-mix the muffins when adding extra ingredients, the muffins should be mixed only enough to blend the liquid into the dry mixture.

INDISPENSABLE IDEA

Try making muffins using fruit flavored yogurt for the liquid for a slightly different taste and when you make muffins bake a double batch and freeze the extras.

Cornbread

Once you have made the cornbread batter there are a variety of ways to cook it: in a square, round or ring-shaped pan, in muffin tins, or in molds that make miniature loaves shaped like a cob of corn. The bat-ter itself can be enhanced with bits of green pepper, onion, canned or frozen corn kernels or fruit such as dried apricots or peaches depen-ding on what food it will be served with.

INDISPENSABLE IDEA

When you cook bacon, save the rendered fat and use it when you make cornbread instead of shortening... it adds a marvelous flavor that seems perfectly suited for the cornbread.

Quick Tea Breads

Quick tea breads are usually baked in a loaf and cut in slices to serve. They are made of a rich biscuit batter with additional flavorings and ingredients. Sweet quick breads are flavored with fruit (bananas, apricots, apples, and so forth) and nuts. Savory quick breads are flavored with onions, zucchini, tomatoes, squash, green peppers and other vegetables. Quick breads gain some of their liquid from the added ingredients so the amount of milk or water used in the batter is normally reduced when these extra liquid bearing ingredients are added. Too much liquid is what causes the indigestible calamity of a soggy, heavy loaf. It's always a good idea to let these breads cook completely before cutting because most of them crumble rather easily.

Pancakes and Waffles

Pancakes and waffles are too often made for breakfast only. These wonderfully versatile breads can also form the base for a wide variety of luncheon and dinner entrees. Virtually any creamed food can be served over pancakes or waffles. In addition, their flavor and texture can be greatly varied by ingredients that are added to the batter before cooking. The amounts for added ingredients given here are based on a batter made with about two cups of flour but adjust the amounts of additional ingredients to suit your taste.

NUTS: Add 1/2 cup of chopped nuts to the batter or sprinkle nuts over the finished product.

APPLE: Add about a cup of grated apple and a little sugar (depending on the tartness of the apple).

PINEAPPLE: Add about 1/2 to 2/3 cup drained crushed pineapple.

BLUEBERRY: Blueberries can be added either to the batter or, in the case of pancakes, sprinkled on after the batter has been poured into the pan, before the cake has been turned.

BACON: About 1/4 cup of cooked and crumbled cooked bacon can be added to the batter before baking.

CORN: Add about 2/3 cup corn kernels.

Once the waffles or pancakes are made, they may be topped with wide variety of toppings from creamed meat, fish, or vegetables, to chili or curries, to strawberries-and-whipped-cream.

Yeast Breads

There are many excellent books on bread making. Baking bread is certainly one of the most satisfying things a cook can do and an area you will want to explore if you have not already done so. Don't be daunted at the prospect of bread making. Follow you recipe directions, take your time, use good ingredients, and you will produce a product you will be very proud of.

Here we will briefly look at ways to make already baked bread distinctive and memorable.

REHEATING YEAST BREADS:

The best way to reheat bread is to put in it a slightly dampened paper bag and then in a 350 degree traditional oven for five to ten minutes (depending on whether you are warming an entire loaf or individual rolls). This method retains a crisp crust.

Microwave reheating warms the bread but changes the texture because some of the moisture is lost in the heating process. If you do use a microwave for reheating, set it at the lowest power.

Alternatively you may wrap the bread in foil and heat either in the oven or in a steamer. Bread may also be warmed directly in a steamer without wrapping but it has to be carefully monitored so that it does not become soggy.

Toasting is a way of reheating, of course, but produces a product quite different from the original.

ENHANCED SLICES:

Spread sliced bread with butter mixed with a little mild mustard.

Sprinkle a generous amount of grated cheese on one slice then put another slice of bread on top add some mustard and cheese and so forth until you've used up all the bread or all the cheese or (ideally) both. Put in a reconstructed loaf back in a regular bread pan or wrap a partial loaf in foil, and heat in a 450 degree oven for about 10 minutes. This same technique can be used with butter and cinnamon-flavored sugar to good effect.

CHUNKY BREAD:

A similar idea is to take an unsliced loaf (perhaps one that you have made), trim the crusts and cut lengthwise through the center in both lengthwise directions and then into large cubes. Pile the cubes loosely into a pan and pour seasoned melted butter over all then heat, uncovered, in a 450 degree oven for a few minutes.

To season the butter try adding grated cheese, minced onion, garlic powder or paste, chopped parsley or chives, or cinnamon sugar. Another possibility is to lightly spread the cubes with soft cheese, devilled ham or a softened liver or chicken pate.

French or Italian Bread

Use one of these spreads described above on the loaf, loosely wrap in foil and warm in a 350 degree oven for about 15 minutes before serving.

INDISPENSABLE IDEA

There are several ways to make exceptionally good garlic bread:

1. Add a mashed clove of garlic to a combination oil made of 1/4 cup olive oil and 1/4 cup salad oil. Warm the ingredients gently before spreading on slices of bread.

2. Spread the bread with soft butter. Peel and score a large clove of garlic and rub the garlic vigorously over the bread. (It takes a rather sturdy bread to survive this.)

3. Mix softened butter with garlic paste which can be purchased either in jars or tubes and spread on the bread.

Sprinkling garlic salt on buttered bread comes in a very poor fourth when put up against these other methods.

CHEESE SPREADS:

Plain or seasoned cream cheese (try seasoning creamed cheese with Dijon mustard or creamy horseradish).

Mix grated swiss cheese with a little Dijon mustard and a bit of sour cream.

Mix any grated cheese with caraway seeds and mayonnaise.

Mix grated Parmesan or Romano cheese (ideally grated from a chunk) with a little butter.

MEAL ACCESSORIES

BUTTER SPREADS:

Combine a half cup of softened butter or margarine with 1/4 tsp. of one or more dried leafy herbs (basil, oregano, tarragon, thyme).

Combine with one or two tablespoons of fresh parsley, chives, or other fresh herb.

Combine with 1/2 teaspoon of paprika, curry powder or chili powder.

Combine with one to two tablespoons of some mild variety of mustard.

SOUR CREAM SPREADS: Almost anything that can be added to butter can be added to sour cream. In addition try combining sour cream with creamed cheese with or without other seasonings.

Hot Rolls

Hot rolls can best be enhanced by varying the spread that is served with them. Using butter or margarine as a starting point, and depending upon what meal the rolls will accompany, make either a savory spicy blend or a sweet spicy blend.

For a savory blend, add your own selection of fresh or dried herbs (don't forget dried onion bits), bacon bits, a bit of mild mustard or a few drops of Worcestershire sauce.

For a sweet blend, mix in a bit of honey or sugar and some of the sweet spices (cinnamon, nutmeg, or allspice for example), a little grated orange rind or a few drops of a fruit syrup.

English Muffins

The English muffin is one of the most versatile of all breads. Although most frequently served with breakfast, it makes an excellent adjunct to any meal and a very good snack on its own. If possible, never buy pre-cut English muffins because it is the hills-and-valleys that can only be achieved by pulling the two halves apart that give it its distinction.

This special surface traps butter, cream cheese, or whatever topping you use while still retaining its crisp, chewy texture.

To make your already-good English muffins even better, here are some not-so-ordinary ways to serve them:

...spread with butter, sprinkle with grated Parmesan or Romano cheese and top with a bit of garlic or onion powder, and pinch of dried oregano, broil until cheese is a little bubbly and slightly browned.

...spread with a thick Italian seasoned tomato sauce, add some grated Mozzarella then top with sliced black olives, bits of anchovy or tuna or pepperoni or cooked Italian sausage and put under the broiler to make an individual "pizza". Cut in wedges to use as an appetizer or canape.

...mix butter or margarine with sugar, cinnamon, and finely chopped nuts and broil till bubbly.

...put two half slices of cooked bacon or a thin slice of Canadian bacon on the muffin, add a thin slice of tomato, and top with a slice of cheddar or Swiss cheese and broil till cheese melts.

...spread a fairly thick layer of tuna mixed with mayonnaise and chopped celery on the muffin, add a ring cut from a whole green pepper and put some peeled, seeded, and chopped tomato in the center of the ring. Put under broiler to warm.

Final thoughts about breads...

Breads are "reputation makers". When you take a loaf of French bread redolent with butter and herbs to a potluck... When you add bits of dried apple to a double batch of muffins and share them with a neighbor... When you entertain with a soup-and-bread buffet featuring three or four unusual breads to accompany the soup... You make it clear that you are a creative cook.

Experiment... try something new from time to time just to see how it tastes. You soon will develop your own bread specialties that will become solid favorites with your family and friends.

COFFEE AND TEA, THE DRINKABLE ACCESSORIES

Coffee is by all measures, the most popular beverage, certainly the most popular non-alcoholic beverage, on at least six of our seven continents.

There are a number of stories about its "discovery" but a favorite is about the Moslem hermit who was having trouble staying awake during his meditations. He spoke about his problem to a passing shepherd who told the hermit about a certain bush that grew nearby. It seems that when the shepherd's sheep ate the berries that the bush produced they became extraordinarily lively and would prance around for hours... even all night. The bush was, so the story goes, the coffee plant with its bright foliage, white blossoms, and green and red berries. We know now that the reason the sheep (and the hermit) stayed awake was that coffee contains caffeine which is a central nervous system stimulant.

Although very popular throughout the Moslem world from about 600 AD, it was not known in Europe until the 1600's. It was first introduced by travellers who had learned to love it while visiting in the Arab countries and brought some back for their own use and to share with family and friends. Colonization by European countries took the coffee bush to parts of the world where it had been unknown before, but where it flourished and eventually exceeded the production of the middle east many times over... Brazil, Jamaica, Java.

In London in 1688, one coffee house was a favorite with merchants and shippers of coffee who eventually pooled their resources to insure (or guarantee to make good) each others' shipments in case of loss. This coffee-house was run by Mr. Edward Lloyd and named for him, Lloyd's. It was this coffee house that was the foundation of Lloyds of London and "insurance" became, and still is, their principle line of work.

The coffee we drink everyday represents a tribute to the international characteristics of life in the twentieth century. If you should ever visit a coffee packing plant you would find yourself surrounded by shipments from the middle east, from South and Central America, from the Caribbean, from Mexico, from Africa, from Hawaii, and from India... and perhaps other places as well.

Unless you prefer one of these varieties unadulterated, what you normally drink is a blend of several, a blend that has been carefully balanced by experts whose business it is to taste, mix, taste, mix, and taste again until they develop just the right combination of flavors.

To give you just one example of this blending, Mocha coffee beans come from the Arabian peninsula. These beans are high in acid and not smooth tasting. When roasted, ground and brewed alone the beverage they produce would seem harsh to most of us. Java coffee, on the other hand, is mild and mellow and very low acid. Taken alone it has a flavor that is too bland for most tastes. However, put the two together, and you have a winner which combines the best characteristics of each and produces a product that is better than either.

An unusual fact about the coffee plant is that it typically bears blossoms, green (unripened) and red (mature) berries all at the same time. This means that it is not possible to harvest the ripened berries by machine and so coffee is hand-picked. The blossoms of the coffee plant are very aromatic and when the coffee is grown near a coastline, it is possible to smell their fragrance well out at sea.

Plants take about five years to mature to the point of being able to produce a commercially usable amount of fruit. The fruit of the bush is called a cherry, and each cherry contains two coffee beans which are removed during initial processing. If your family uses a pound of coffee a week, you are consuming the production of about fifty coffee bushes each year because about two thousand beans are required for a pound of roasted coffee and this is about the annual crop of one plant.

Coffee beans are stored unroasted because once roasted they have a relatively short life. Grinding also diminishes the time that coffee is at its best. Vacuum packing makes it possible to keep ground coffee available on our supermarket shelves at all times, but once you open the vacuum package the clock starts running and within a short time (weeks) you will notice a deterioration in the taste. Even freezing will not stop this flavor loss completely.

Many people who really love coffee prefer to buy roasted coffee beans before they are ground and grind them at home on an as-needed basis. This is the way to have the very best coffee in the world.

There are a variety of ways to brew coffee from the mundane to the exotic... here are the major methods:

Boiling... In the chapter on camping you will find a description of the way to make boiled coffee. While this method has its staunch advocates, you must be told that for coffee purists this is an inconceivably bad way to prepare their favorite beverage because boiling will cause the essential oils present in the brew to become bitter.

Percolating... This was a very popular method for decades but has the same drawback as boiling, the coffee takes on a bitter taste. For some people accustomed to drinking percolated coffee, this is bitterness is the way "real coffee" tastes.

Dripping... First there was the three part metal coffee maker: put coffee in the middle part, pour boiling water into the top part and let the brewed coffee drip into the bottom section. Then there was the Chemex and its cousins, a heat-proof glass container shaped like an hourglass with a cone of filter paper put in the top, finely ground coffee added and boiling water (actually 190 degree water was recommended) poured over. And most recently, the automatic drip coffee maker complete with timers, warmers, and simplicity of use.

In Europe you will find little packets of coffee in filter paper, not unlike tea bags, that are used to make individual cups of coffee. From Italy comes the espresso machine which forces steam under pressure through pulverized beans to produce a very strong, dark beverage which is usually served in half-sized (demi-tasse) cups.

INDISPENSABLE IDEA

To make instant coffee taste almost like fresh-brewed, make it in a pan, bring it to a boil and let it stand for two or three minutes before serving.

Mix instant coffee granules, sugar, and cinnamon and use it as a sprinkled-on topping for chocolate, coffee, or vanilla ice cream.

Tea has its own special history.

According to Chinese tradition some five thousand years ago the water available to the court was undrinkable and had to be boiled. One afternoon the emperor was resting in an outside courtyard and watched as the wind blew some leaves from a convenient tea bush into a boiling pot of water that just happened to be nearby (just why it was nearby is not made clear in the story). He tried the brew (or more likely had the Imperial Taster try it) and pronounced it heaven-sent.

Our word, tea, takes its derivation from the Chinese Amoy dialect which calls the plant "t'e" which is pronounced as "tay". The Japanese word for tea "cha" is the root from which languages such as Russian and Turkish have developed. From these two Asian countries, love of tea has spread throughout the world.

Although there are extensive varieties of tea to choose among, all are taken from one plant the *Thea* (or *Camillia) sinensis,* an evergreen that can grow to about thirty feet in height but is usually kept trimmed to a much shorter height. Tea plants grow either in fields or in terraced hillsides and require both a warm climate and heavy rainfall (from 90 to 200 inches a year).

The finest quality leaves are the first one or two tiny leaves that appear at the end of each individual branch. These special leaves are picked several times a season. Leaves further down on the stem are less choice. The principal differences among teas are determined by the way the leaves are treated and finally blended.

There are three broad categories of teas: black, green, and oolong.

Black teas are produced when the freshly picked tea leaves are allowed to ferment, usually on cement floors under damp cloths. The oxidation of the leaves when treated this way softens the tea's natural astringency. Tea brewed from black tea is a reddish-brown in color and is the most popular type of tea in western countries. Darjeeling and Assam (from India), and Lapsang Souchong (from China) are black teas.

Incidentally, when you see "Pekoe" on a label, it refers to the size of the tea leaf used rather than its flavor or place or origin (pekoe are the largest, orange pekoe are smaller leaves).

Green teas are steam processed and not fermented. The brew is yellow to greenish-yellow in color and is favored in the Orient, particularly in Japan where a ceremony called "cha no yu" has been perfected around the process of graciously brewing, serving, and drinking tea.

Oolong teas are semi-fermented and what might be described as a compromise between black and green in flavor.

India, China, and Sri Lanka are important producers of tea and each country's particular climate produces noticeable differences in the tastes of their teas. The taste of the tea leaves can vary significantly from harvest to harvest within a given year and from year to year depending on weather and rain conditions. For this reason teas are blended from several pickings to develop a uniform and predictable flavor.

The first tea merchant opened his shop in London in 1657 and within a few years tea had taken hold as England's most popular drink, so popular in fact that the government levied a tax on tea to protect the coffee industry. Tax or not, tea continued to grow in popularity both in England and in its American colonies. By the 1800's tea popularity was at its height and shiploads of dried tea leaves travelled from the Orient to Atlantic ports for sale. Even today, taken on an international scale, tea is the most popular beverage in the world.

Brewing tea is simple but for a good brew certain rules must be followed.

First, the tea pot should be clean and rinsed with boiling water (to pre-warm the pot).

Second, an ample amount of tea should be used (one rounded teaspoonful of loose tea or one tea bag per cup of water).

Third, start with cold tap water and heat it just until it boils then pour it on the tea. Let the tea steep for five minutes and stir it before you pour.

If tea produced this way makes it seem too strong for your taste, brew the tea by these rules but dilute it by adding hot water to your cup before you drink it... the tea won't be as strong, but all of the flavor will be there.

Tea is often taken just "as is" but it is also served with various "accessories" itself. Lemon is a favorite addition and serves to sharpen the flavor of the tea whether it is served hot or iced. Milk (not cream) is another addition that is favored by some because it cuts the acid quality of the taste. Sugar does more than simply sweeten tea, it also enhances its flavor.

INDISPENSABLE IDEA

Unless your iced tea is so strong that you want to dilute it, make ice cubes from left over brewed tea of the same strength to chill without diluting this warm-weather favorite. The same can be done when making iced coffee.

Various nationalities also have preferred ways for drinking their tea. The Japanese ceremonial tea service has already been mentioned. In Turkey and other parts of the Middle East, tea is served in small glasses, very sweet and sometimes flavored with mint. Russians like a strong tea which is brewed and then kept warm in and served from a large samovar, often sweetened with jam and a slice of lemon. Typically the British like milk in their tea and usually put the milk into the cup first then pour in the tea. Americans have developed a taste for teas enhanced with spices, oranges, and other flavors.

However you like them, tea and coffee are definitely in our lives to stay.

CONDIMENTS, ENHANCING ACCESSORIES FOR ANY MEAL

Finally let us look at that other segment of the food accessory scene... condiments, those little extras that can add so much to any meal.

Catsup

Catsup (or as it is sometimes spelled, ketchup) is a sauce with a long and colorful history... far more exotic than the ubiquitous sweet-bland, bright red tomato catsup of the fast food emporiums would suggest. Originally brought back from India by the British, catsups have traditionally been made, and are still made by curious cooks, from walnuts, mushrooms, grapes, berries, and, in the eighteen century at least, from stale beer and chopped anchovies! Catsup has never been as popular in other parts of the world as it is among English-speaking peoples for some reason.

If you would taste a catsup worth remembering, forget the bottles of flavored tomato sauce on the supermarket shelves and take a day in late summer to make your own... you won't believe the difference and you'll never be satisfied with commercial catsup again.

The word catsup or ketchup, incidentally, is derived from the Malay "kechap" and the Chinese " koetsiap" which means a pickled fish brine.

INDISPENSABLE IDEA

To spice up too-bland catsup, mix it half and half with Taco sauce.

Mustard.

Mustard has been in use as a condiment for centuries and is found in a wide range of ethnic cuisines. Starting from the simple round mustard seed which is ground into a fine powder, the flavor of the mustard sauce is controlled by the liquid used (water, milk, beer, wine), the other seasonings that are added (salt, herbs, capers, garlic, apricots, and many others), and the way the sauce is processed (how long it is left to mellow before using).

If you make your own, and that is a very satisfying thing to do, be sure to allow time for the flavors to meld together and mellow out a bit before you plan to use it.

If catsup is the condiment of choice among the British and North Americans, then mustard must be considered the favorite condiment of the French and they not only consume a lot but also make a lot in their famous mustard factories in Dijon. (The only museum in the world dedicated to mustard is, not surprisingly, in Dijon.)

Mustard seeds are of three kinds: white (actually beige in color), brown, and black. American-style mustard, the familiar hot-dog mustard, is made primarily from white mustard while Dijon is made from black or brown. Mustards may be either smooth or grainy with the graininess produced by adding some crushed mustard seeds to the final mixture.

American-style mustard tends to be mild in taste, bright yellow (because of the turmeric added), and smooth. Delicatessen-style mustards usually are spicier and grainier. French Dijon mustards are pungent and spicy and smoother in consistency. German mustards come in two general types, hot or slightly sweet. English mustard is just plain strong and a straight-forward mustard flavor. Chinese mustard is the hottest of all and often very spicy as well... best to use sparingly. Not strictly speaking a mustard sauce is the "mosdarda" of Italy which is a fruit-mustard combination.

INDISPENSABLE IDEA

Spread a tablespoon of grainy deli-type or German mustard on a thick slice of French bread and broil until bubbly. Put the toasted bread on top of a bowl of French onion or split pea soup.

Add a bit of Dijon mustard to the cheese sauce you serve with cauliflower or broccoli.

Add mustard to melted current jelly for a ham glaze or spread it on a thick slice of ham before you broil it.

Mix mustard with softened butter or margarine and use it on broiled fish or chicken.

Other Entree Sauces.

Steak sauces such as Worcestershire, A-1, Heinz 57, and many others are all dark sauces of varying thickness and flavors which are used to enhance meat dishes. Worcestershire sauce, the grandfather of all steak sauces, was developed by an Englishman living in India and is a combination of soy sauce, vinegars, anchovies, tamarinds, molasses and a wide assortment of herbs and spices. When its developer brought it back to his home in, you guessed it, Worcestershire, England, it was almost instantly popular and has remained so ever since its introduction. Worcestershire sauce is thin in consistency compared to other steak sauces which, allowing for their various formulas, are more similar to catsup than to Worcestershire.

Soy sauce, that essential of all Oriental cooking, has moved into a permanent place in western kitchens as well. Perhaps the only drawback to soy sauce for some people is that it has an extremely high proportion of salt (sodium) per volume and if you are concerned with the amount of sodium in the meals you prepare, you should keep that in mind. In addition to the traditional soy sauce, "light" soy sauce is also available which has about 40 percent less salt than the original, but even so the sodium is still high. (Ordinary salt is 40 percent sodium.) Sodium notwithstanding, soy sauce is essential in the preparation of almost all oriental foods and is also used in marinades and other western dishes as well. Soy sauce is made from slightly fermented soy beans. American manufactured soy sauces tend to be somewhat sweeter than oriental imports, Japanese sauces are more flavorful and Chinese soy sauces may seem stronger to the casual user.

Tabasco sauce is strictly an American product, in fact "Tabasco Sauce" is exclusively produced in New Iberia, Louisiana (although there are several other hot pepper sauces available that have a similar although not identical taste). Tabasco sauce is hot. Until you develop a taste for it, use it carefully... it is sold in a dropper bottle for a very good reason. On the other hand, a drop or two or several of Tabasco sauce can spark up a wide variety of foods from scrambled eggs to beef stews. Just use sparingly and taste carefully as you go because once added there is no way to retreat from the hot Tabasco taste. Replace your Tabasco sauce regularly. Because so little is used by most cooks, we tend to keep a partially used bottle around for a long time. Like all things, Tabasco changes in time and takes on a dull brown color. Although still safe to use it just isn't as good as a sauce from a fresh bottle will be.

MEAL ACCESSORIES

Chili sauces and *barbecue sauces* are in a middle ground between the blandness of commercial catsup and the hot-ness of chili pepper sauces such as Tabasco. Barbecue sauces can be purchased ready-made but are often made by the cook according to a "secret" formula that can make a cook's reputation. Chili sauce is a tomato based sauce, thinner and not as smooth in consistency as catsup and also contains ground tomatoes, onions, peppers and so forth. Chili sauce is not as popular as catsup but it should be because it can be so good.

Many other foods can be considered food accessories... the vast numbers of pickles, mayonnaise and other egg-based sauces, and all of the other sauces too: mint, orange, cranberry, and butter-based sauces of all kinds. Be experimental... buy and try commercially prepared condiments, and try making some of your own as well. Many are not difficult although they may be time-consuming. All are fun to try and satisfying to produce.

Chapter 8:

KITCHEN WISDOM

What follows are some ideas that may make your time in the kitchen easier and more pleasant. They have all been tried and found to work. Some of the standard kitchen "tips" that you see in a lot of books have not been included because they have been tried and found not to work. Why don't you try some of these ideas yourself and see what you think.

ALMONDS. You can, in fact, save some money if you buy unblanched almonds and blanch them yourself, and it's relatively easy to do. Simply bring to a rolling boil enough water to cover about a half cup of nuts. Drop the nuts in the water, remove from heat and allow the nuts to stay in the hot water for about a minute. Remove with a slotted spoon and drain on paper towels. Sometimes you can squeeze each nut between your thumb and forefinger and have it slip right out of the skin. More often you will have to use a paring knife to assist the nut out of the skin. Although simple to do, this job is time consuming and unless you have an (unpaid) kitchen helper, you would probably be better advised to spend a little extra money and buy blanched almonds.

ANCHOVIES. If you find anchovies just too salty, you can take some of the saltiness away from them or other salt-cured foods by either soaking or rinsing in cold water. The longer the water is in contact with the food, the more salt will be removed.

APPLES. To keep the skins of baked apples intact, make slits around the apple in several locations with a sharp knife. As soon as the liquid produced by cooking has an easy way to escape, it will not burst its way out elsewhere.

To keep a cut apple from browning, flow some bottled lemon juice over the cut surface then wrap the partial apple tightly in plastic wrap.

To keep apple pieces or slices from browning, cut them into a bowl containing either lightly salted water or some lemon juice mixed with water.

ARTICHOKES. To improve taste, texture, and color of artichokes, soak them for about a half hour in a bath containing a tablespoon of vinegar per quart of water and then cook as usual.

ASPARAGUS. If asparagus becomes wilted, stand it vertically in a pan or jar in about two inches of very cold water. Cover with a plastic bag and fasten to the jar with a rubber band. Put in the refrigerator for one to two hours before you cook.

AVOCADOS. To speed the ripening process of those rock-hard avocados that are sometimes all you can find in the produce department of your local supermarket, put the avocados in a brown paper bag and leave them at room temperature for a day or two. When ripe store in the refrigerator to keep from ripening further.

As soon as you cut the avocado pour bottled lemon juice on any portion you don't plan to use, leave the seed in the unused portion, wrap tightly with plastic wrap and store in the refrigerator. It will keep without darkening for at least a few days.

BAKING. If you have a problem with uneven baking, it may be because you are placing pans too closely together. To allow for adequate circulation of heated air in the oven, allow at least two inches of space between all pans, and also between pans and the walls of the oven. Remember that ovens cook with convection heat which means the heat is circulated as the warm air rises and the cooler air falls. This circulation is very important to satisfactory baking.

To keep dough from sticking, spray countertop and rolling pin with oil spray before you start to roll it out.

If your cakes and other baked goods are lop-sided, put a carpenter's level on one of the oven shelves and see if perhaps the stove is tilted. If it is, most stoves have adjusting devices built into their bases that can be used to level them.

BAKING PANS. Breads and pies bake best and will have the best crust when baked in a dark colored pan that absorbs heat well. On the other hand, cookies, biscuits, and cakes do better in a shiny pan that reflects the heat for a more delicate browning of the crust.

BAKING POWDER. Baking powder loses its effectiveness over time. If you have some on hand of unknown age, a quick way to see if it will still do the required job is to put 1/2 teaspoon of the baking powder into 1/4 cup of hot tap water. If the water bubbles, the baking powder is still fresh enough to use. If not, you'll be happier with a new box.

BANANAS. In the 1940's and '50's there was a radio advertisement that advised cooks that "bananas are a product from the very, very tropical equator, so you should never put bananas... in the refrigerator". Because the jingle had to rhyme something with "equator", a generation of cooks was raised with that warning ringing in their ears. Except for the fact that the skins will turn brown, there is no reason not to refrigerate ripe bananas. It is, in fact, the only way you can keep them for any length of time.

If you suddenly have an abundance of ripe bananas that you are not going to be able to use or refrigerate, put them in your blender with a little lemon juice and make a puree that you can freeze and use for banana bread or topping sometime later.

BARBECUES. Warm the basting sauces you use on meat because a cold sauce will slow the broiling.

To see how hot the coals are, place the palm of your hand about at the level the food will be. If you can slowly count to 8, the heat is "low". If you can only count 5 it is medium, and if you can only make it to 3, it's ready to go. Be careful not to burn your hand!

BEETS. To keep fresh beets from losing their deep red color when they are cooked, leave about two inches of stems attached to the beets, put about 2 tablespoons of vinegar in the cooking water, and peel the beets after they are cooked.

BISCUITS. If you want soft-sided biscuits, bake them in a pan with sides and put the formed biscuits close together. If you prefer crusty-all-around biscuits, bake them on a cookie sheet or other sideless pan and place them apart from each other.

BOUILLON and **CONSOMME.** If you don't like the taste of canned bouillon and consomme but appreciate the convenience, try simmering it with some additional seasonings, especially some extra onion, garlic, celery, and/or bouquet garni for about five minutes. It will significantly improve on the "canned" taste.

BRAISING. When you braise meat, you dredge it in seasoned flour, brown it quickly and then add enough liquid to just cover the meat and slowly cook it in a covered pan. Cooked in too much water, a meat dish will boil rather than braise and the flavor will be in the broth, not the meat. To prevent a braised meat dish from boiling, take a piece of heavy foil and shape it into a shallow flat bowl. Place it on top of the meat, under the lid of the pan with the open side up. As the steam rises from the cooking meat dish it will collect on the lid and drop into the foil bowl. This will keep the braising liquid from thinning out. Keep an eye on things though and make sure that the braising liquid doesn't evaporate entirely.

BREAD CRUSTS. You can style your own bread crusts according to your family's preferences.

For a soft, well-browned but not shiny crust, before baking brush the loaf with a tablespoon of melted butter.

For a crisper and shinier crust, bake the loaf for 20 minutes then remove from the oven and brush with an egg white that has been beaten with a tablespoon of water and return the loaf to the oven to finish baking.

For a slightly browner and slightly crisper crust, brush after 20 minutes with a whole egg beaten with a tablespoon of milk.

BREADING. If you find you need bread crumbs and have no dry bread on hand to make them, consider using dry cereal. Make it into crumbs either in your blender or by putting the flakes between sheets of waxed paper and crushing with your rolling pin.

To make a breaded coating that sticks to the food try this: Take three shallow dishes and put flour in the first, beaten egg in the second, and seasoned bread crumbs in the third. Coat each piece of food first with the flour, then with the egg, and finally with the seasoned crumbs. Place the breaded food in the refrigerator for at least an hour and for as long as four hours before cooking to "set" the coating.

BROILING FISH. The broiler pan should be hot before you introduce the fish. Put the pan in the oven and heat it thoroughly then quickly brush it with oil and place the fish, skin side down, on it. The fish will cook perfectly and it will be easy to remove it from the pan.

BROILING MEAT. Spatters from broiling meat are a nuisance and potentially hazardous because of the fires they sometimes start. To avoid excessive spatters try putting some slices of bread in the bottom part of the broiler to absorb the fat as it melts. Some people recommend putting a cup of water in the broiler pan but this produces steam and that is something you don't particularly want when you are broiling.

BROWN SUGAR. If it becomes too hard to use, put it in a jar with a tight lid and a wedge of fresh apple. It takes about a day to become soft enough to use. To prevent brown sugar from drying out in the first place, keep it in an air-tight plastic bag, or in a jar or container with an air-tight lid.

BUTTER. If your recipe calls for unsalted butter and you have only salted butter on hand, remember that in each half pound of salted butter there is about 3/4 teaspoon of salt and reduce the salt you add to your recipe by that amount.

CABBAGE. To soften cabbage leaves before making stuffed cabbage rolls, remove the core from a large head of cabbage and place it in pan of hot water. Heat the water to not-quite-boiling. Remove the cabbage and carefully peel off the outer leaves that have softened. Put the head back in the water, bring the water back to a simmer and repeat until you have enough cabbage leaves.

CAKE. After you have poured the batter into the cake pan, lift the pan about six inches above the counter and drop in gently. This will dislodge air bubbles in the batter that would otherwise bake into the finished cake as holes. Don't do this with angel food or other chiffon cakes however because they depend on the air trapped in the batter to raise properly.

Do you have trouble getting a baked cake out of the pan? Try placing the pan on a wet towel when you take it from the oven. When the pan is cool, shake the pan gently and the cake will slip right out. (This works because the cake steams a little in the pan when the pan is cooled quickly on the wet towel. The steam separates the cake from the pan.)

If you want to have a cake ready in a hurry, pop it into the freezer while you make the frosting. By the time you have the frosting ready to go, the cake will be cool and ready to slip out of the pan. Quickly cooling a cake this way is not going to raise the temperature of your freezer significantly.

If you have a problem with cakes that like to stick to the cooling rack, try putting down a hard-finish paper towel before you put the cake on the rack. It will cool just as well and will not stick to either the cooling rack or the towel. It also helps to spray the cooling rack with vegetable oil spray. (This problem can also be caused by cakes that are not baked quite enough, or cakes that you bake in your microwave because the tops of these cakes are still moist.)

CAKE FROSTING. It is generally most convenient to frost the cake on the serving plate to be used but hard to do the job without frosting getting all over the plate. To keep the serving plate clean, place several strips of waxed paper around the edge of the cake between the cake and the plate. When you have finished frosting the cake, carefully remove the strips and the cake plate will be pristine.

To make a "perfect" frosted cake, do it in two stages.

First brush the loose crumbs from the sides of the cake then spread on a thin base coat of the frosting. Dip your spatula in water from time to time to keep it smooth. Let the frosting set up slightly then apply the finishing coat. It will go on much more easily and the finished product will be just what you had hoped it would be... beautiful, elegant, and delicious!

Incidentally, if the cake has a filling, be sure not to spread the filling all the way out to the edges or it will run over when the top layer is added. Spread it out and leave about a half inch all the way around the cake for the filling to spread. The frosting will fill in any gaps.

CAKE LAYER SPLITTING. To split evenly a layer into two parts, there are two things you can do:

You can place a row of toothpicks around the outside of the cake at the point you want to make the cut then, using a serrated blade slicing knife, cut through the cake.

Possibly easier and more reliable is to loop a length of waxed dental floss around the outside of the cake at the point you want the cut then cross the ends and pull gently but firmly. The floss will cut right through the cake.

Layer cakes just don't go together well if the layers are not even and an oven that is slightly off level will produce an uneven layer every time.

Until you can have the stove leveled you can "adjust" layers by just simply trimming the uneven portion off. The layers will be thinner but work just as well in the cake.

CARAMEL COATING. To coat a mold evenly with caramel (cooked sugar) keep the mold in very hot water while you prepare the caramel. Pour the melted sugar immediately into the mold and swirl it around. A four cup mold can be coated with 1/2 cup sugar mixed with 2 tablespoons of water. The mixture must be watched and stirred very gently but constantly. The more brown the mixture, the stronger the flavor. Do not ever leave this mixture while it is cooking... just let the phone ring!

CARROTS. Don't store unwrapped carrots in the same storage container as ripe fresh apples. The apples give off ethylene gas that causes a "ripening" process in all fruits and some vegetables and in carrots can result in the carrots acquiring a bitter taste.

CAULIFLOWER. Cauliflower will stay white if you cook it with a strip of lemon peel.

CHARRED PANS. To remove badly burned-on food from a pan, try this: Scrape away as much of the burned-on food as you can, then fill the pan with cold water, add a cup of salt and let it soak overnight. In the morning bring the water slowly to a boil and allow it to boil gently for about fifteen minutes. Turn off the heat and let the water cool. Pour it out and finish cleaning with a scouring pad. The burned food should come off easily.

CHEESE STORAGE. You can prevent most molds from growing on cheese in your refrigerator if you store the cheese in an air-tight container in which you have also put a folded-up paper towel that has been saturated with white vinegar. The vinegar provides an acidic atmosphere that the molds don't like a bit.

CHEESECAKE. When you take a cheesecake out of the oven be sure to keep it away from drafts and cold places while it cools. Too abrupt a temperature change can cause the top of the cheesecake to crack. If that should happen in spite of your best efforts, you can make it look as though you planned it that way by covering the top with a pretty arrangement of fruit... strawberries, pineapple sections, apricot halves... whatever you have on hand. If you should also happen to have some jelly that you can melt with a little water and pour over the top, you have a cheesecake that any deli would be proud to sell. (Who knows, maybe a cheesecake with a cracked top was the "inspiration" for strawberry cheesecake!)

CHOCOLATE. To melt chocolate smoothly and easily, wrap the solid chocolate in foil and place in a 300 degree oven for about 10 minutes. Check to see if it is melted and if so simply scrape into your mixture. A variation on this theme is to put the foil-wrapped chocolate in the basket of your steamer over simmering water. Both of these methods keep the chocolate from separating and also makes clean up easier.

If, in spite of all your best efforts, chocolate you are melting over-cooks and becomes hard and "dull" looking, put the pan on very low heat and beat in one tablespoon of shortening at a time until you have restored the shiny, smooth look of perfectly melted chocolate.

COCONUTS. To use a fresh coconut, puncture the "eyes" with an ice pick or clean screwdriver and drain out the coconut milk. Put the whole coconut in a shallow pan and bake for about an hour at 350 degrees in your oven. When it is cool enough to handle hit it a good whack with a hammer and the shell will part. The meat then has to be pulled out in chunks with a table knife. Peel off the brown skin. To shred, put chunks of coconut with a little of the milk into your blender or food processor. Store shredded coconut in the refrigerator.

COOKIES. For a quick pretty glaze for sugar cookies, beat an egg white until just frothy and brush over the unbaked cookies. Sprinkle with sugar and bake. This will give your cookies a shiny, sweet crust.

When rolling out cookie dough to cut, try using a thin dusting of powdered sugar instead of flour on the board. The flour tends to make the dough thicker and heavier while the dusting of sugar will help the cookie to brown evenly.

To keep cookie dough from sticking to your cookie cutters, first be patient and wait until the dough is chilled before you roll it out. Then dip each cookie cutter in oil before pressing into the dough and the cookies will cut cleanly. This oil treatment is particularly useful when using cutters with intricate designs or cutters made of plastic. (You can also spray the cutter with oil spray.)

You can keep your slices of refrigerator cookies perfectly round when you cut them if you put the dough into empty frozen juice cans and chill. When you are ready to bake, just cut the bottom off the can and use it as a pusher to move the dough forward as you slice the cookies.

CORNED BEEF. If your corned beef turns stringy and dry after cooking, it may be because you removed it from the cooking liquid too quickly. To keep the piece of meat tender and juicy, cook completely and let it cool in the liquid until it is warm rather than hot, then remove and slice for serving.

CORNSTARCH. The sauce for cornstarch thickened dishes such as stir-fry vegetables or sweet-sour pork will retain the right consistency if you do not cook at too high a temperature. Cooked with too much heat, the high-acid content of these dishes may cause the sauce to thin out after an initial thickening. The best thing to do is bring to a quick boil over direct heat and then finish cooking in a double boiler over just-simmering water. A second possibility is to use flour and cornstarch in a half-and-half combination. A sauce thickened this way will not be as clear as a sauce thickened with just cornstarch but it will tolerate high heat better.

CORNSTARCH PUDDINGS. If you want to keep a soft surface on puddings thickened with cornstarch (packaged pudding mixes are thickened with cornstarch), simply press a piece of plastic wrap down on the top of the cooked pudding before it cools. On the other hand, some kids think the "skin" is the best part... all a matter of taste.

CRUDITES. For making those raw vegetable, low calorie favorites with the dieting crowd, keep in mind these things:

Carrot strips will curl if placed in a bowl of water with ice cubes. Use your vegetable peeler to make the thin strips and gently wind them around your finger before putting into the ice water.

Radish roses will also open up in iced water. Keep the slices from the sides of the radishes very thin for this to work the best.

Cauliflower, turnip, jicama and other firm white vegetables will stay white and crisp if you cut it into a bowl of water with lemon juice added.

Celery will crisp up if placed root end down in a container of salted water.

For really crisp cucumber slices, slice the cucumbers into a light salt-water solution and refrigerate for an hour or so then rinse well with cold water. Slices can be dressed up a bit by scoring the length of the cucumber with the tines of a fork, or by leaving thin strips of the dark green peel at intervals around the cucumber before slicing.

Consider the idea of putting the dip for the crudites in a hollowed out green or red pepper.

CUSTARDS. If you plan on turning out the custard (for a creme brulee for example), you will have better luck if you bake it in a metal container because the metal cools more quickly than glass and will release more easily.

DRIED BEANS. Cooked dried beans are excellent food and very nutritious as well as being high in fiber. Many of the problems people have in digesting cooked dried beans can be avoided if you soak the beans in cold water overnight, drain them in the morning and discard the water. Add fresh water to cook the beans, and when they are tender discard that as well. The enzyme in the beans that can cause problems dissolves in the water and the problems goes down the drain with the discarded water.

DRIED FRUITS. To make them easier to cut, repeatedly dip your knife or scissors in very hot water. Spraying with kitchen oil spray also helps to keep dried fruit from sticking.

EGG WHITES. Freeze extra egg whites in ice-cube trays and store in air-tight plastic bags until you need them.

A major exception to the kitchen rule that "freshest is best" are egg whites that you want to whip because less fresh egg whites whip higher and hold the air better than new egg whites. Keep separated egg whites in a loosely covered container in the refrigerator or, better yet, in the freezer as this will allow some of the fluid to evaporate and they will become stiffer when beaten.

Always let egg whites warm to room temperature before beating to maximize the volume of the beaten eggs.

To stabilize beaten egg whites (for souffles for example), add about 1/2 tsp. of cream of tartar for each two egg whites.

EGG YOLKS. If you have extras they can be stored in two ways.

For use within a day or two, rinse a small storage container with water and gently slide the yolks in then add enough water to cover the yolks.

For longer storage you can freeze the yolks. For each six yolks, Gently stir in not more than a half teaspoon of honey. Freeze in a small container. The yolks can be thawed and used as you would fresh yolks and will not be sticky.

When adding egg yolks to a hot component of a dish, always warm the egg yolks a bit with some of the hot mixture before pouring the them in. If you simply add the cold egg yolk to the hot component, you will in a sense "scramble" the egg and cause the dish to curdle.

EGGS, BROKEN. If you should drop an egg, you can have a real mess on the floor. You'll be surprised how easily you can clean that mess up if you cover it with a light layer of salt and let it rest for 15 or 20 minutes. The whole thing will wipe up beautifully... well, it will at least come up relatively intact and a little detergent and water will finish the job.

EGGS, HARD COOKED. To successfully remove shells from hard-cooked eggs, after the necessary cooking time drain away the hot water. Shake the eggs in the pan vigorously to crack the shells in many places. Cover the eggs with cold water and add several ice cubes. Remove the shells as soon as the eggs are cooled.

If you hard-cook several eggs for use over a number of days, remove the shells and store the eggs in a jar of water in your refrigerator.

EGGS, POACHED. To keep poached eggs intact, add enough cider vinegar so that you can just notice the change of water color. Bring the water to a gentle boil and crack each egg into a small flat dish. Gently slide the egg into the boiling water. With a spoon immediately push the egg white toward the yolk. When the egg is firm, remove with a slotted spoon and put into a bowl with cold water. Eggs can be poached well in advance, kept in a container of cool water and simply warmed for 30 seconds in simmering water before serving.

EGGS, SEPARATING. Eggs will separate most successfully when they are cold so when you need stiffly beaten egg whites remember the rule: separate cold, beat at room temperature. (And don't let a speck of egg yolk mix in with the whites!)

EMERGENCY FOODS. Power blackouts, snow storms or a variety of other not-so-pleasant events can make an emergency supply of food welcome. If you have most of the following on hand all the time, you can manage, if not extravagantly, at least adequately. Remember you want to maintain daily intake of the major food groups.

> Protein Sources:
> > Canned fish, chicken, corned beef, luncheon meat
> > Canned prepared dishes (chili, corned beef hash, whatever your family specially likes)
> > Cheese spread in jars
> > Canned condensed soups with meat
> > Peanut butter
>
> Carbohydrate Sources:
> > Cereals

> Crackers
> Canned brown bread
>
> Fruits and Vegetables:
> > Canned whole or pieces
> > Juices
> > Dried fruits
>
> Milk Sources:
> > Canned evaporated milk
> > Dry milk
>
> Other possibilities:
> > Flavored gelatin
> > Mayonnaise (in small jars)
> > Coffee and Tea

A small propane camp stove or Sterno cooker may be a valuable asset in power-out emergencies and of course are battery powered flashlights and radio.

ENERGY SAVERS. A double-boiler (bain marie) will heat more efficiently if the water in the bottom pan has a little salt added. This is because salt water boils at a slightly higher temperature than plain water.

If you can use some hard cooked eggs and will be cooking something in a double boiler for 10 to 15 minutes, put the eggs to be hard boiled in the lower part to cook at the same time.

Preheat the oven only when necessary. Many dishes don't require preheating (baked potatoes, for instance). Don't forget to turn the oven off when you take the finished dish out... an easy thing to do!

If you are going to cook one part of the meal in the oven, try to plan your menu so you cook other parts of the meal at the same time and/or cook something for use another day.

Don't play peek-a-boo with baked dishes. Preheat the oven, put the dish in, set the timer, and don't look again until the timer goes off. If you have reason to doubt the timing of the recipe, set the timer for ten minutes or so less than the recipe says.

If you use an electric stove: After a stew or soup has finished cooking, turn off the heat. The burner retains enough heat to keep the dish warm but let it cool a bit to a comfortable temperature for eating.

Cool hot foods in the refrigerator before freezing and thaw frozen foods before cooking (unless the frozen food package says not to thaw). Any exchange of heat-for-cold or cold-for-heat is going to take energy.

You can lose a lot of cooling from your refrigerator because of a worn out or improperly fitted door gasket. For a quick check, take a dollar bill and close the refrigerator door on it. If you can easily pull the bill out, the gasket is too loose and you are losing cold air all the time.

FISH. Try thawing packaged raw frozen fish in a bowl of milk. The milk seems to definitely improve the taste of the fish and make it seem fresher somehow.

When poaching fish that you would like to serve whole either hot or chilled: put a piece of oiled parchment paper or heavy foil in a pan long enough to hold the fish flat. Place the whole fish carefully in the pan. Add cold liquid to cover (hot liquid can cause the skin to split). After poaching, let the fish cool completely in the liquid before you try to remove it from the pan. When you are ready to take it out, firmly grasp the foil or parchment paper with one hand on each side of the fish and lift it out to a waiting platter.

FLAMBE. There is just one key to successful flaming of dishes... the liquor must be warm. Cold food will cool even pre-warmed liquor so work fast or warm the dish slightly in a 250 degree oven for about 10 minutes then add liquor. If you cannot pre-warm the food, the alcohol should be warmed until hot to the touch and set aflame as soon as it is placed on the dish to be served. Do not allow the liquor to boil because that will cause the alcohol (which is what burns) to evaporate.

To make the flames last longer, sprinkle the dish with a little sugar before flaming.

Whenever you serve a dish flambe, stand back slightly and be very careful not to have your face (or your hair) too near.

FLOURS. The all-purpose white flour you see on supermarket shelves is a compromise. It is a combination of hard wheat which is best for bread making because it has more gluten, and soft wheat which has less gluten is best for cakes, biscuits and other products where a soft crumb is desirable. By combining both, all-purpose flour really does neither job very well. If you are serious about baking, look for flour that is suited for each job: flour from hard wheat is usually called baker's flour or bread flour, flour from soft wheat is called cake flour or pastry flour.

FOOD-GRINDERS. When you have used a food-grinder you can get all of the ground material out and make the grinder much easier to clean if you run a slice of bread through it before dismantling.

FRENCH FRIED POTATOES. For crisp french fries: Be sure the pieces are thin and all the same thickness. Soak the pieces in ice water for an hour before frying (to remove excess starch). Dry the pieces very carefully (water left on will spatter in the hot oil and also cause the piece to steam rather than fry). Make sure the oil is the correct temperature. Fry the potatoes in two stages... first fry for about 2 or 3 minutes then remove and drain on paper towels and cool, then put them back in the oil and fry until golden brown. Put in a brown paper sack, if you sprinkle with a little salt and shake, you will drain and salt in one action.

FRUIT. If you have unripened fruit that you would like to hurry up a bit, try putting it in a plastic bag that has been punched with a few holes. The ethylene gas that the fruit produces naturally will speed the ripening but be contained in the bag, the holes will allow for some air circulation. (Ripe apples can be used as a ripening accelerator with any fruits.)

You can keep your hands from being stained with fruits you are preparing if you spray you hands with oil spray before you start.

GELATIN DESSERTS AND SALADS. Do not use fresh pineapple in gelatin dishes. Pineapple is a member of the bromeliad family and contains an enzyme that will interact with the protein of the gelatin and prevent it from setting. Canned pineapple has been cooked and this enzyme is destroyed with heat so it works without jelling problems.

Here are some ideas for quick ways to remove gelatin desserts and salads from molds (none absolutely guaranteed but all worth a try...). Rinse the mold out with cold water before introducing the gelatin mixture, or spray the mold with baking spray (use only when a clear surface on the jelled dish is not required because a residue of oil may be left). When it is time to unmold, place the mold on a warm wet towel briefly and/or shake the mold from side to side to loosen the jelled mixture (this works best with small individual molds).

GRAHAM CRACKER CRUMBS. You can buy graham cracker crumbs but it is so simple to make them that buying them ready-made seems pointless. Just put the crackers into your blender a small amount at a time. Turn the blender on and off and the pieces will move down into the blades. If you don't use a blender, put the crackers in a plastic bag and crush with your rolling pin. You can even use the plastic bag as a container to add the butter and sugar to make up the crumbs for a graham cracker crust and toss the whole messy thing out when you are finished rather than dealing with yet another mixing bowl.

GRATING. When grating cheese or other sticky foods, if you brush the grater lightly with oil before you start it will be much easier to clean when you are finished.

HOLLANDAISE SAUCE. Curdled hollandaise can usually be rescued this way: Start with one cup of curdled sauce. Heat the container of your blender with very hot water and drain it well. In the container combine 1 egg yolk, 1/4 tsp lemon juice and 1/4 of the curdled sauce. Turn the blender on and then off immediately. Turn on again to its lowest speed and start at once to slowly pour in the rest of the curdled sauce. Turn off as soon as all of the remaining sauce has been introduced. The sauce should have smoothed out. If it has not, try blending for a second or two more.

HONEY. When measuring honey, molasses, or syrup, rinse your measuring cup with hot water first and you can easily pour the sticky liquid out after measuring.

ICE CREAM. Spray kitchen oil spray over anything used to make or handle ice cream (ice cream maker, scoops, freezer trays...) and the ice cream will be much easier to handle.

JARS. Opening tightly sealed jars can be a frustrating, and muscle wrenching, experience. When all else fails (or even before all else fails), turn the jar upside down in a pan of water and pour in hot water to just cover the lid. Heat the water to boiling, take the bottle out and (with a towel or hot pot holder) twist the lid off. The heat will cause the metal to expand enough to make it come off easily.

KITCHEN TOOL (The Best). Your most versatile, useful, and least expensive kitchen tool is found at the end of each arm. Don't hesitate to use your hands and fingers when you cook... your fingers are more sensitive (to test doneness for instance) than any tool, more flexible (for buttering baking pans for instance) than any brush, more gentle (for separating eggs for instance), and just generally very useful. Rinsing in the sink or wiping on a handy towel will keep them clean and ready to use for the next job.

LEMONS. Store whole lemons in a jar of water in the refrigerator and you will find that you get more juice from them. Soaking for 10 minutes or so in hot water before juicing will also increase the juice you get.

Remove the zest from a lemon (zest is the yellow portion with none of the white attached) and store it in a jar containing about a half cup of vodka. The zest will not spoil and will be available for use whenever you need a little bit and the vodka will pick up a lemon flavor (use it in dessert sauces, or in seafood dishes).

LETTUCE. You can revive wilted lettuce in two ways. Submerge it in a bowl of water to which you have added a couple of tablespoons of lemon juice and place the bowl in the refrigerator for an hour.

A second way is to put the head under running hot water for several seconds then place it in a bowl of ice water to which has been added a couple of tablespoons of white vinegar.

MELON BALLS. To make perfectly round melon balls, put the cutting edge of the melon ball cutter flat on the fruit and press down firmly, then turn your wrist and scoop out a luscious globe of fruit. Pressing the cutter in firmly forces the fruit into the top of the cutter to make the ball. If you take the cutting edge into the fruit at an angle (which would seem to be the sensible thing to do), you will end up with one flat side on the ball.

MERINGUES. If you have trouble removing crisp meringue shells from the baking paper, try this: after baking the meringues at the lowest possible temperature for about 2 hours, lightly moisten the underside of the paper with cool water. Slide your spatula carefully under the meringue and it should lift off easily and in one piece.

When using a meringue topping on a pie, always spread meringues all the way out to the pie crust and "attach" it to the crust all the way around. This will keep the meringue from shrinking. Turn off the oven and open the door a crack when the meringue has finished browning and let the pie cool slowly in the oven. This will keep the meringue from cracking and "weeping".

MILK. Before scalding milk, rinse the pan with cold water. The pan will be much easier to clean.

Many recipes still call for scalded milk although the technique was originally necessary before milk was pasteurized (it killed bacteria and microorganisms in the milk). The benefit from scalding milk now is that by warming the milk first, cooking times are shortened and also because heating the milk makes its flavor more pleasant and mellow.

MOZZARELLA. To cut even, slim slices of mozzarella or other semi-soft cheese, dip the knife in hot water before each cut.

MUFFINS. If you find that your muffins brown around the edges before the centers are cooked, try partly filling one section of each muffin pan with water. The extra steam will keep the edges from over-cooking.

MUSHROOMS. Never store mushrooms in a plastic bag because they quickly become slick and unpleasant. They keep best either in a brown paper bag (with the top folded down) because the brown paper absorbs the moisture that the mushrooms produce. They can also be stored in a rigid sided storage container with the lid attached loosely but the paper bag really works best.

Fresh mushrooms are those whose caps are completely closed, no gills showing, and they are what you should buy.

To keep mushrooms white while you are sauteing them, either add a half teaspoon of lemon juice to each half cup of melted butter or (if you are sauteing whole caps), saute the tops of the caps first and fill the cap with lemon juice while the top is sauteing.

MUSTARD. To keep an opened jar of mustard fresh tasting longer, place a thin slice of lemon on top before your close the jar tightly.

NUTS. After you have shelled nuts by hand you may have the sneaking feeling that some of the shells may have gotten in with the nuts... to put your mind at rest, just put all the nuts into a bowl of water. The nuts will sink to the bottom and the shells will float on the top. Just skim them off. Don't leave the nuts in the water very long though.

You can toast raw nuts yourself this way: place the nuts on a cookie sheet or other shallow baking pan and brush lightly with a mild cooking oil (or put some oil on your hands and rub the oil lightly on the nuts). Place in a 350 degree Fahrenheit oven and turn the nuts from time to time until they are uniformly golden brown. (Sprinkle with salt after toasting if you wish.)

Another way to roast and salt your own nuts successfully is to lightly whip an egg white in a fairly good sized bowl, pour the nuts into it and shake them around. Scoop them out of the egg white and scatter on a baking sheet. Sprinkle with salt (use a coarse grind if you can find it) and bake at 300 degrees Fahrenheit until the nuts are golden brown.

You can chop nuts in a blender without ending with clumps of nuts lumped together if you add about a tablespoon of flour to the nuts before you grind them.

To keep nuts (or raisins, currents, or other fruit) from settling to the bottom of a baked dish, mix them with some of the flour called for in the recipe before stirring them into the batter.

OIL. When using hot oil to cook, having the oil hot enough is very important... especially when cooking oriental foods. There are four ways to check the heat.

The first is, of course, to use a deep-fat frying thermometer. Other, less precise but quite usable include:

Hold your hand about two inches above the oil (do not let water drop into the oil or it will spatter). If you can hold your hand there comfortably, the oil is not hot enough.

Put a bamboo chopstick or skewer in the oil. If bubbles gather around it right away, the oil is hot; if not, remove the chopstick and let the oil heat a while longer.

And finally, drop a small piece of raw vegetable into the oil. If it sizzles and moves vigorously in the oil, the oil is hot enough to use.

Oil used for deep frying can be reused if you are careful. After each use, strain through a fine strainer. To remove unwanted odors and tastes, heat the oil and cook slices of raw potato or a bunch of parsley and then strain. The oil cannot be used indefinitely, of course, but you can extend its life this way. When it becomes quite cloudy, however, the best thing to do is start over.

OLIVES. You can extend the refrigerator storage time of an opened can of olives if you immediately pour any you cannot use into a glass jar, fill the jar with vegetable oil and cover the jar. The oil will preserve the olives and can be used in cooking when the olives are gone. If you prefer not to use this much oil because of dietary or other reasons, simply leave the olives in their original brine and flow a layer of oil on top.

ONIONS. If an onion seems too strong to use raw on a sandwich or in a salad, place the slices in a bowl of water to which you have added about 1 teaspoon of sugar per cup of water. Let the slices soak for about an hour and you will find they have given up their harshness.

Rub your hands with parsley after cutting up onion and the onion smell will vanish.

When cooking onions and garlic together, always cook onions first then add the garlic. Flavor of each will be kept separate and the garlic will not become bitter.

ORANGES. You can peel oranges more easily if you blanch them in boiling water for about 5 minutes. Cool, and the peel slips right off. You can increase the amount of juice you get from an orange if you press on it as you roll it around your countertop before cutting. Also, keep in mind that thin skinned oranges are better for juice, while thick skinned oranges are better for eating in sections.

OVEN TEMPERATURES. Possibly the most common cause of baking failure is an oven thermostat that is inaccurate. It is well worth the small investment it takes to buy an oven thermometer so that you will know, when you set the oven thermostat for 350 degrees Fahrenheit, exactly what heat your oven reaches. If it doesn't give you a reliable 350 degrees, either have the thermostat adjusted or adjust your cooking times accordingly. Temperatures too low can cause cakes to fall and pie shells to be soggy. Temperatures too high can cause cakes to brown on the surface before the center is cooked and pie shell edges to burn.

PARSLEY. To keep parsley fresh for up to two weeks, trim a half inch from the bottom of the stems and place the whole bunch in a covered jar that contains enough water to keep the stems wet. Every few days, cut off another half inch or so because the stems will tend to seal and stop taking up water if you don't.

Another way to keep parsley fresh in your refrigerator is to put the bunch in a plastic bag with a quarter of an apple.

PASTA. If you add a tablespoon of olive oil and a teaspoon of salt to the cooking water for pasta you will: keep the water from boiling over, keep the pasta from sticking together, and add a bit of flavor to the pasta.

When the pasta is cooked to al dente, drain immediately and, if you are not going to use right away, put it in a bowl of ice water to stop the cooking. You can reheat either in the oven, in a steamer or in a microwave oven.

PEARS. Pears ripen from the inside out. If you wait until the fresh pear looks perfectly ripe on the outside, it may well be over-the-hill on the inside.

PIE CRUST. To make the best pie crust keep these things in mind: use the full amount of shortening called for, chill the shortening before adding and keep everything as cold as possible while you work with it; don't add too much ice water (water causes the gluten in the flour to stretch and the crust will be tough); handle the dough as little as possible to keep it cool and to avoid stretching the gluten; roll in one direction at a time, always out from the center of the dough to the edges.

There are a variety of ways to prevent soggy bottom crusts. Here are some that work well:

Brush the bottom crust with lightly beaten egg white. The coating will help prevent the absorption of liquids from the pie.

With fruit pies you can put a thin layer of fine cookie crumbs in the bottom. (This is especially good for an apple pie... try using ginger cookies!)

Another possibility is to sprinkle the bottom crust with a combination of equal parts of sugar and flour before adding the filling... or spread a layer of finely ground nuts on the bottom (particularly good with cream pies).

For quiches or other custard filled pies, put the bottom layer in a 450 degree Fahrenheit oven for 10 minutes before filling. This "sets" the crust and keeps it from absorbing the liquids from the filling.

PIES. To keep unfilled pie shells from bubbling up and becoming not only unattractive but also possibly unusable, prick the bottom and sides of the shell very generously with a fork. Be sure to go all the way around the line where the bottom of the pan meets the side. More trouble, but additional assurance of a flat bottomed pie shell, is to put a circle of baking parchment or waxed paper against the flat pie dough and then pour a thick layer of dried beans on the paper. The weight of the beans will keep the bottom flat. These beans can be used over and over for this purpose. (Rice can also be used as a weight.)

To keep the top firmly attached to the shell of a two-crust pie, try moistening the edge of the shell with beaten egg yolk or even milk before pressing the edges together. A fluted edge is simple and attractive, just pinch the two layers of dough between your thumb and forefinger and bend the fold slightly. Takes a little (but truly not much) practice to perfect and is a nice skill to have.

PIMENTOS. Often a recipe calls for a small amount of pimento and you find that the left over portion spoils quickly in the refrigerator. Since pimentos are relatively expensive, save them for later use by pouring off the liquid they are packed with and replace it with a mild cooking oil (or freeze).

PINEAPPLE. If the fresh pineapple you choose turns out not to be sweet enough for your taste, remove the top, peel it and slice it. Put the slices in a pan with water just to cover and add sugar to taste. Bring just to a boil then immediately remove from the heat, cool slightly and refrigerate until well chilled. You'll never know that it wasn't a perfect fresh pineapple.

POPCORN. Popcorn will pop better if you store it in the freezer and pop while frozen.

POTATOES. Potatoes will stay white after you peel them until you are ready to cook them if you cut the pieces into a bowl to which has been added either a teaspoon or so of lemon juice or vinegar, or some salt. Don't let the potatoes soak in the water too long though because they can lose a lot of their excellent supply of vitamin C if they do.

Removing a number of baked potatoes from the oven can be a bit of a problem since it is very easy to touch the oven and find yourself with an unpleasant burn. If the potatoes are a suitable size, not too big, try baking them standing on end in a muffin tin. That way you can remove six at a time and you'll find they will bake just a little faster that way too.

RED CABBAGE. If the color fades when you cook red cabbage it is because your cooking water is too alkaline. Make the water more acid by adding a little vinegar or lemon juice.

RICE. For fluffy rice, cook the rice completely. When it is done, remove it from the burner and put a crumpled up paper towel on top of the rice and replace the lid. Let the rice rest while you assemble the rest of the meal. The paper towel will absorb all of the extra moisture and the rice will be neither sticky nor dry.

ROASTS. Roasts cook better (in fact "roast" rather than steam) when the meat is elevated from the bottom of the pan. If you do not have a roasting rack, you can still accomplish this by one of two ways, either rest the roast on a layer of canning jar rings, or make a grid of carrots and put the roast on that (this latter idea will, of course, also add some additional flavor to the drippings).

SALAD BOX. You can save a lot of time in meal preparation with a "salad box" in your refrigerator. Buy a plastic storage box with an air-tight lid and keep in it a variety of vegetables washed and trimmed and ready to go into a salad. This way you can take out the one box and be ready to start your dinner salad instead of several plastic bags that have to go back and forth. The box can be filled when you return from shopping and are putting the fresh vegetables away.

SALT WATER. To keep many fruits and vegetables from discoloring after they are peeled, cut the pieces into a bowl of salted water (about 1 tablespoon to a quart of water). This works well with apples, peaches, pears, potatoes, avocados, and other produce.

SALT, TOO MUCH. If you have oversalted a dish it is sometimes possible to save it by adding a teaspoon each of vinegar and sugar to the dish and simmering for a short while. It will not taste quite the same but in an emergency you might try it.

Slices of raw potato will also absorb extra salt. For a stew or soup, you can try adding thick slices of potato. The potato will attract and hold some of the excess salt and can be removed before serving the dish.

SHRIMP. If you are using canned shrimp you can improve the taste a lot by rinsing well with cold water and then soaking in a little white wine before using.

SLICING. Don't use your egg slicer only for slicing eggs... it works just as well on any soft food: mushrooms, olives, small potatoes and so forth.

SOUFFLES. The trick to producing a no-fail souffle is simply this: cool the white sauce mixture before adding to the beaten egg whites. Cook the sauce then remove it from the heat and add the egg yolks. Mix all together well and then let it cool... really cool... until you can comfortably hold the pan on the palm of your hand. Then add to the beaten egg whites. It goes without saying, (or does it?) that any souffle must be served as soon as it is ready... have everyone at the table ready and waiting before you remove the souffle from the oven.

If for some reason you cannot put a prepared souffle directly into the oven, cover the uncooked souffle with a bowl and leave at room temperature. If the egg whites were sufficiently whipped and folded into the mixture it can be successfully held for about 20 minutes... long enough for a forgotten oven to preheat!

To ensure the highest souffle, do not over-do folding the egg whites into the sauce mixture. Too much mixing will break down the protein molecules of the egg whites and allow the captured air to escape.

SOUP. Freeze extra soup in empty, rinsed out milk cartons. The rectangular shape stores efficiently in your freezer and the cartons are easy to empty. Staple the top closed and tape it with freezer tape to prevent freezer burn.

STEAKS. To test for doneness, don't cut into the steak because you will lose the juices. Instead practice doing it by touch. Press the raw steak before you cook it and impress on your mind how it feels. When you have cooked the steak take it out an press it and remember how the raw steak felt. If it still "gives" quite a bit, it is rare. If it feels firmer with more resistance when you press, it is medium. And if it is very firm, it is well done. This technique takes a bit of practice but once you get the "feel" of it, it works wonderfully.

STOCK. Whenever you steam or boil green or yellow vegetables, save the cooking liquid and accumulate it in a container in your refrigerator. When you accumulate about a quart, put it on and reduce it to about half by boiling in an uncovered pan. This stock can be used to make soups or stews that are both flavorful and nutritious. A simple but delicious creamed soup can be made using this as a base, adding 1/3 cup of dried milk for each cup of stock and thickening as you would for a thin white sauce (2 tablespoons of butter and 1 tablespoon of flour for each cup of liquid); add some leftover vegetables for texture and sprinkle a little nutmeg or paprika on top.

Always start a meat stock in cold water to pull the most juices possible from the meat. If you start it in hot water the meat seals itself and keeps the juices in.

Another thing to keep in mind when making meat based stocks is to always add a couple of tablespoons of vinegar to the water. The vinegar makes the broth a little acid and causes some of the calcium in the bones to be released which makes the stock much more nourishing.

Keeping stocks of all kinds (chicken, beef, vegetable, fish) on hand in the refrigerator is a splendid idea and you will find yourself using them in a variety of ways. To keep stock fresh and safe to use, however, you should take it out once a week, bring it to a full boil and boil for 3 to 5 minutes. Cool and return to the refrigerator. This process also integrates the flavors that you have added to your refrigerator "stock-pot" during the week.

If clear stock is important (for consomme for instance) there are two ways to accomplish it.

To make a clear broth start from scratch, start with cold water and quickly bring the chicken or meat to a boil. Pour off the water. Add fresh water and bring up to a simmer. Do not let the stock ever come to a rolling boil but continue to simmer gently.

To clarify stock that has been boiled, lightly beat an egg white with 1 tablespoon of cold water and the crumbled shell of one egg for each quart of stock to be clarified. Add to the stock and heat to boiling. Boil for 2-3 minutes and remove from heat. Do not stir, but allow to settle for a half hour. Carefully pour the stock through a sieve that has been lined with wet cheesecloth.

Stock can be frozen in your ice cube trays and stored in sealed air-tight plastic bags until you need it. Always bring the frozen stock to a boil before adding though because the freezing process causes some separation of the stock components.

SUGAR. If you have a recipe that calls for "superfine" sugar, just put regular granulated sugar in your blender and turn on and off several times until the sugar granules have been reduced in size slightly.

TEA. To make your own (inexpensive) spiced tea simply pour loose tea leaves into a jar that has a tight lid. Add your favorite spices singly or in combination and store for a couple of weeks before using. Some flavors you might try include cinnamon stick, whole allspice, dried orange or lemon rind, cardamom, pieces of vanilla bean... just use your sense of smell and imagination.

To remove tea stains from the inside of your teapot or cups, rub with a paste made of baking soda and water.

To make crystal clear iced tea try either of these techniques:

To each cup of cold water add 3 teaspoons of tea leaves. Put in the refrigerator and let it infuse for a day or two. Add water to taste and serve on ice.

A second way to make clear iced tea is to make Sun Tea by using the same proportions of tea to water and putting the mixture in a covered jar that you can place outside in the sun. The tea will have steeped in about 3 hours.

TOMATOES. An easy way to remove seeds and liquid from most varieties of tomatoes is to make a series of vertical slits in the tomato, hold it over the sink and squeeze, twisting it a little bit in your hand. This will not remove every seed, but it will leave you with mostly pulp and a tomato intact enough to peel easily.

Tomato slices will hold their shape better if you slice the tomato vertically instead of horizontally because the natural strength of the tomato goes in that direction. The slices look a little different but are much easier to handle.

TURKEY. To keep cooked turkey from drying out, soak a kitchen towel in warm water and wring it out. Put it firmly around the turkey while the turkey is still warm and then refrigerate. (This will work when the meat is still on the bird as well as for sliced meat.)

VEGETABLES. To keep vegetables fresher longer in your refrigerator, keep them dry as well as cool. Don't let water collect in the cooler drawers of your refrigerator and line the drawers with paper towels, thin sponges, or the plastic liners designed specially for this purpose. Herbs such as parsley will keep best if they are put in a covered jar with about two inches of water.

Any vegetable that has a tight thin skin over a juicy interior (peaches, pears, apricots, tomatoes, to name a few) can be easily peeled if they are blanched in boiling water for a while you slowly count to 10 (about 30 seconds).

WHIPPED CREAM. You can keep whipped cream for use over 2 or 3 days if you use light corn syrup for sweetening.

(You may see some recommendations for using dissolved gelatin, but the end-product is not like regular whipped cream.)

For topping winter pies such as pumpkin or apple, try using rum for flavoring the whipped cream instead of vanilla... a real enhancement!

WHITE SAUCE. A simple memory device for preparing white sauce at the right consistency is: 1-2-3. For each cup of milk use 1 tablespoon of flour for a thin sauce, 2 tablespoons of flour for a medium sauce, and 3 tablespoons of flour for a thick sauce. (Use 2 tablespoons of butter or margarine for any thickness.)

WHOLE WHEAT BREAD. Because there is less gluten in whole wheat flour than in all-purpose white enriched flour, you will find that baking whole wheat products will involve you with a few problems not found otherwise. Here are some suggestions for solving those problems:

Insufficient rising:
Water used may not be warm enough. Try adding a little more salt or use a little more sweetening agent. Simply allow the dough to rise longer (in a warm place away from drafts).

Too bland:
Add a little more salt, or a little more sweetening

Crust is too dark and hard:
Cut back on honey, molasses, or other sweetening. Check oven temperature, may be too hot. Bake for a shorter length of time.

Crust is too light and soft:
Check oven temperature, may not be getting hot enough. Add a little more sweetening. Extend the baking time.

Loaf is too dry and hard:
Use a lower oven setting and/or bake for a shorter length of time. Flour may be extra dry, judge by feel as you knead whether to add more liquid. Don't add extra yeast to speed rising time (it tends to make the bread dry and hard).

Loaf is tough and too chewy:

Adjust baking time (test for doneness by thumping loaf and listening for a hollow sound), tip the bread out of the pan and see if the bottom crust is brown and firm.

Add gluten flour to the mixture a little at a time until you find the amount that makes your bread turn out just as you and your family like it.

WINE. Leftover wine can be used in soups, stews or salad dressings. To save for a cooking purpose such as one of these, try pouring a thin coating of vegetable oil over the top, it will keep the wine fresh longer (but no longer suitable for drinking!).

ZEST. The zest of any citrus fruit is the outermost part that holds the color. If your recipe calls for zest there are two ways to prepare it. To grate the zest, use the smallest holes on your grater and turn the fruit often so that you don't pick up any of the bitter white pith that lies between the zest and the fruit segments. To cut strips of zest, use your sharpest paring knife (or a sharp vegetable peeler) and take off the zest with as little pith as possible. If you do take some of the pith, simple scrape it off with a spoon before cutting into slender strips.

PRONUNCIATION GUIDE

Amaretto (ah-marh-EH-toh)
Anisette (AN-ih-seht)
Brulee (brooh-LAY)
Calvados (kahl-vah-DOHS)
Chartreuse (shar-TROOS)
Cointreau (KWAHN-troh)
Creme (krehm)
Creme de cacao (krehm deh keh-KAH-oh)
Creme de cassis (krehm deh KAH-see)
Creme de menthe (krehm deh MAHNT)
Crudite (kroo-dih-TAY)
Curacao (KOOR-eh-sow)
Drambuie (Dram-BOO-ee)
Entree (AHN-tray)
Fines herbes (feen UHRBZ)
Fiori d'Alpi (fee-OH-ree DAHL-pee)
Flambee (flahm-BAY)
Frappe (frah-PAY)
Framboise (frahm-BWAHS)
Frangelico (frahn-JEHL-ih-coh)
Goldwasser (GOHLD-vah-ser)
Grand Marnier (grahnd mar-nee-YAY)
Jagermeister (YAY-ger-my-ster)
Kahlua (kah-LOO-ah)
Kirschwasser (KERSH-vah-ser)
Kummel (KYOO-muhl)
Liquore (lih-KORE-eh)
Maraschino (mar-ahs-KEE-noh)
Neufchatel (noo-shah-TEL)
Ouzo (OO-zoh)
Pate (pah-TAY)
Picon (pih-KONE)
Pina colada (PEEN-ya coh-LAH-dah)
Prosciutto (proh-SHO-toh)
Puree (pew-RAY)
Quatre spices (KAHT-tehr spees-eh)
Sabra (SAH-brah)
Saute (saw-TAY)
Schnapps (schnahps)
Slivovitz (SHLIH-voh-vihts)
Strega (STREH-gah)
Vermouth (vehr-MOOTH)

INDEX

-A-

INDEX

-B-

-Y- -Z-

Author's Note and Acknowledgements

I was fortunate enough to have been born into a family of good cooks going back at least three generations and I have been enthusiastic about cooking since grade school days. Later I trained and earned my living for many years as a librarian. That combination of inclination, training, and experience has led me to accumulate thousands of handwritten and typed three by five cards, and to fill many notebooks with recipes, notes, ideas, and just general information about foods and cooking. This collection of data is the basis for this book just as it has been the basis for the other writing and lecturing that I have done in recent years. As I said in my note at the end of THE COOK'S BOOK OF ESSENTIAL INFOR-MATION, if I could give a separate acknowledgement and thanks for each bit of information contained in those files and notebooks I would, but it just isn't possible to do so. Again, I hope that all of the people who have contributed in any way will accept my deepest appreciation for making this book possible.

SOURCES FOR MORE INFORMATION

Almost every food product has its own producer association or advisory board whose purpose it is to promote the use of their product. Quite often, therefore, they have an active public relations and publications program. There are a great many of these associations already, and every year produces even more.

There are two excellent publications that include producer associations in their listings. The first is the ENCYCLOPEDIA OF ASSOCIATIONS published by Gale Research Associates Company in Detroit. This multi-volume set is revised and republished annually and is a standard source of information about many kinds of associations. A new title that also contains a comprehensive list of organizations is INSTANT INFORMATION by Joel Makower and Alan Green (Prentice Hall, 1987). Both of these titles should be available at your local public library and the reference librarian will be glad to help you find what you need in them.

In addition to producer associations, food processing and manufacturing companies are another good source of ideas and recipes. If you are looking for addresses for food processors and manufacturers, there are again two good places to start. The first is the THOMAS REGISTER OF MANUFACTURERS another multi-volume set that has been around for many years. It is not the easiest reference book in the world to use, so don't hesitate to ask your librarian for help if you want some assistance with it. Simpler to use, although not as complete, is the annual NATIONAL DIRECTORY OF ADDRESSES AND TELEPHONE NUMBERS which should also be available at your library.

Watch the food section in your local newspaper. Often you will find short notices about companies who are offering recipe booklets or other informational material that can be ordered either without charge or for some nominal fee to cover postage and handling. Labels on products also frequently give an address that you can write for product information or recipes.

The following short list includes a variety of non-governmental sources for further information.

American Cultured Dairy Products Institute
888 16th Street NW
Washington DC 20006

American Sheep Producers Council, Inc
200 Clayton Street
Denver, Colorado 80206

American Viticulture Area Association
c/o Guenoc Winery
P O Box 1146
Middletown, California 95461

Bacardi Corporation
Box G 3549
San Juan, Puerto Rico 00936-6207

California Olive Industry
P O Box 4098
Fresno, California 93744

California Prune Board
World Trade Center
San Francisco, California 94111

Calorie Control Council
5775 Peachtree-Dunwoody Road, Suite 500-D
Atlanta, Georgia 30342

Campbell Soup Company
6200 Franklin Boulevard
Sacramento, California 95824-3412

Champagne News and Information Bureau
220 East 42nd Street
New York, New York 10017

Chocolate Manufacturers Association of the US
7900 Westpark Drive, Suite 514
McLean, Virginia 22102

Food Processors Institute
1401 New York Avenue NW, Suite 400
Washington DC 20005

Fresh Garlic Association
P O Box 2151
Gilroy, California 95021

General Foods Corporation
250 North Street
White Plains, New York 10605

General Mills, Inc.
9200 Wayzata Boulevard
Minneapolis, Minnesota 55426-1306

Halibut Association of North America
309 Maritime Building
911 Western Avenue
Seattle, Washington 98104

Herb Society of America
2 Independence Court
Concord, Massachusetts 01742-2501

Nabisco Foods
River Road and DeForest Avenue
East Hanover, New Jersey 07936

National Broiler Council (chickens)
1155 15th Street NW
Washington DC 20005

National Soft Drink Association
1101 16th Street NW
Washington DC 20036

Oregon Fruit Products Company
P O Box 5283
Salem, Oregon 97304

Quaker Oats Company
W Merchandise Mart
Chicago, Illinois 60654

R. T. French Company
1 Mustard Street
P O Box 23450
Rochester, New York 14692

Spice Islands -- Specialty Brands
633 Battery Street
San Francisco, California 94111-1809

Swans Down Cake Flour
P O Box 60296
New Orleans LA 70160

Washington State Fryer Commission
15403-B 1st Avenue South
Seattle, Washington 98148

Wine Institute
165 Post Street
San Francisco, California 94108

ORDER FORM

SUMNER HOUSE PRESS

2527 West Kennewick Avenue
Suite 190
Kennewick, Washington 99336

Please send me:

———— copies of
THE COOK'S BOOK OF INDISPENSABLE IDEAS
at $9.95 each

———— copies of
THE COOK'S BOOK OF ESSENTIAL INFORMATION
at $9.95 each

Postage and handling $2.00 for each copy.
(For shipments to Washington state addresses please
add 78¢ sales tax.)

I understand that if I am not fully satisfied I may return the book(s)
within 30 days for a full refund.

Name: _____

Mailing Address: _____

City/State and Zip: _____

A GREAT GIFT IDEA FOR BRIDES...BIRTHDAYS... GRADUATES...CHRISTMAS

SUMNER HOUSE PRESS

2527 West Kennewick Avenue
Suite 190
Kennewick, Washington 99336

I would like to order copies of the books noted below to be sent to the people whose addresses I have listed below. I have enclosed $9.95 plus $2.00 for postage and handling for each copy I have ordered. (For shipments to Washington state addresses please add 78¢ sales tax for each copy.)

COOK'S BOOK OF INDISPENSABLE IDEAS
COOK'S BOOK OF ESSENTIAL INFORMATION

Book Title: _____

Name: _____

Mailing Address: _____

City/State and Zip: _____

Ship to receive by (date): _____

Gift card should say: _____

Book Title: _____

Name: _____

Mailing Address: _____

City/State and Zip: _____

Ship to receive by (date): _____

Gift card should say: _____

My name is: _____

Mailing Address: _____

City/State and Zip: _____

YOUR COMPLETE SATISFACTION IS GUARANTEED!

ORDER FORM

SUMNER HOUSE PRESS

2527 West Kennewick Avenue
Suite 190
Kennewick, Washington 99336

Please send me:

———— copies of
THE COOK'S BOOK OF INDISPENSABLE IDEAS
at $9.95 each

———— copies of
THE COOK'S BOOK OF ESSENTIAL INFORMATION
at $9.95 each

Postage and handling $2.00 for each copy.
(For shipments to Washington state addresses please
add 78¢ sales tax.)

I understand that if I am not fully satisfied I may return the book(s)
within 30 days for a full refund.

Name: _____

Mailing Address: _____

City/State and Zip: _____

A GREAT GIFT IDEA FOR BRIDES...BIRTHDAYS... GRADUATES...CHRISTMAS

SUMNER HOUSE PRESS
2527 West Kennewick Avenue
Suite 190
Kennewick, Washington 99336

I would like to order copies of the books noted below to be sent to the people whose addresses I have listed below. I have enclosed $9.95 plus $2.00 for postage and handling for each copy I have ordered. (For shipments to Washington state addresses please add 78¢ sales tax for each copy.)

COOK'S BOOK OF INDISPENSABLE IDEAS
COOK'S BOOK OF ESSENTIAL INFORMATION

Book Title: _____

Name: _____

Mailing Address: _____

City/State and Zip: _____

Ship to receive by (date): _____

Gift card should say: _____

Book Title: _____

Name: _____

Mailing Address: _____

City/State and Zip: _____

Ship to receive by (date): _____

Gift card should say: _____

My name is: _____

Mailing Address: _____

City/State and Zip: _____

YOUR COMPLETE SATISFACTION IS GUARANTEED!